THE TRIAL OF DONALD RUMSFELD

THE TRIAL OF DONALD RUMSFELD

A PROSECUTION BY BOOK

Michael Ratner
and the Center for Constitutional Rights

THE NEW PRESS

NEW YORK
LONDON

Requests for permission to reproduce selections from this book
should be mailed to: Permissions Department, The New Press, 38 Greene Street,
New York, NY 10013.

Published in the United States by The New Press, New York, 2008
Distributed by W. W. Norton & Company, Inc., New York

LIBRARY OF CONGRESS CATALOGING-IN-PUBLICATION DATA

Ratner, Michael, 1943–
  The trial of Donald Rumsfeld : a prosecution by book / Michael Ratner and
the Center for Constitutional Rights.
     p. cm.
  Includes bibliographical references.
  ISBN 978-1-59558-341-3 (hc.)
  1. War crimes—United States—History—21st century.   2. War
criminals—United States—History—21st century.   3. Torture—Government
policy—United States.   4. War on Terrorism, 2001–   5. Rumsfeld, Donald,
1932– I. Center for Constitutional Rights (New York, N.Y.)   II. Title.
  D804.5.W65R38   2008
  973.931092—dc22

                                                        [B]   2008016248

The New Press was established in 1990 as a not-for-profit alternative to the large,
   commercial publishing houses currently dominating the book publishing
industry. The New Press operates in the public interest rather than for private
gain, and is committed to publishing, in innovative ways, works of educational,
cultural, and community value that are often deemed insufficiently profitable.

                            www.thenewpress.com

                  Composition by Westchester Book Composition
                       This book was set in Stone Serif

                   Printed in the United States of America

                        2 4 6 8 10 9 7 5 3 1

Contents

Acknowledgments

Putting together a book of this sort requires the help of many people. The Center for Constitutional Rights would like to thank everyone who contributed to the effort. Claire Tixeire's research, writing, and mastery of the material brought shape and clarity to the work. Esther Wang kept constant track of all the pieces and propelled the project to completion. Thank you to Jen Nessel for making it happen. Thanks to interns Garrett Wright, Sinan Kalayoglu, Anna-Delia Papenberg, and Jayna Turchek for all of their work. Special thanks to Diane Wachtell and Priyanka Jacob at The New Press, as well as to Andy Hsiao and André Schiffrin for initiating the project.

CCR would also like to give credit to all the people who worked on the original German lawsuit against Donald Rumsfeld, Alberto Gonzales, and the other high-ranking officials responsible for constructing and carrying out the war crimes detailed in this book: Wolfgang Kaleck of the European Center for Constitutional and Human Rights; Michael

Ratner, Peter Weiss, Scott Horton, and Hannes Honecker of RAV; Claire Tixeire and the team at the International Federation for Human Rights (FIDH); and everyone else who worked to bring justice for the victims of the Bush administration's programs.

THE TRIAL OF
DONALD RUMSFELD

The Trial

1

Opening Statement

This is an unusual trial. It is occurring in the form of a book that lays out the evidence that high-level officials of the George W. Bush administration have ordered, authorized, implemented, and permitted war crimes, in particular the crimes of torture, and cruel, inhuman, and degrading treatment. I am Michael Ratner, an attorney and the president of the Center for Constitutional Rights (CCR). With others at CCR, I will present this case against what we call the "torture defendants."

We are proceeding by way of a trial-by-book, because at this point there appears to be no other means of holding high Bush administration officials criminally responsible for their war crimes. Certainly no one in the administration is willing to do so; until recently, the Department of Justice was headed by one of the accused, Alberto Gonzales, and until recently, the Department of Defense was headed by another of the accused, Donald Rumsfeld. Even if both of these two defendants were no longer in government, no criminal actions would be filed.

The government did launch several investigations and released numerous reports following the wake of the public outcry over the Abu Ghraib torture and abuse. The Taguba, Schlesinger, and Fay-Jones reports, together, criticized the interrogation methods and confirmed that the entire chain of command was responsible for the torture and abuse at the Iraqi prison.

But the Bush administration is not about to investigate itself.

Efforts made to begin investigations in other countries so far have been unsuccessful. The major effort by the Center for Constitutional Rights in Germany failed. A case filed in France in October 2007 was also not successful. Despite Rumsfeld's presence in Paris, the French prosecutor failed to arrest him or issue a warrant to obtain his testimony. Sadly, efforts to get Congress to hold the Bush administration accountable, even a Congress controlled by the Democrats, also have not been successful. There have not even been serious hearings on the responsibility of high Bush administration officials for the planning and implementation of the torture program. To make matters worse, the Senate confirmed someone for Attorney General, Michael Mukasey, who refuses to admit that waterboarding is torture.

In these circumstances there is an obligation to set forth the facts, give the defendants their chance to defend, and make a determination of whether or not they are guilty. We cannot and should not sit idly by while high-level officials in the most powerful country in the world are allowed to torture with impunity. Think about the message that sends to other countries that contemplate using torture: it is a green light to do so. Think about what it means if U.S. soldiers are captured: the U.S. will have no moral or legal authority to complain. How could we object if a U.S. soldier is waterboarded? Torture is difficult to eliminate; it becomes impossible if the country that could set the moral example refuses to do so. That is why we must hold those responsible for torture accountable. We cannot put the genie back in the bottle. We cannot go back in time and stop what has occurred. Perhaps we can deter future conduct if we send a message to the world that torturers, like the pirates of old, are enemies of all humankind and will be brought to justice no matter their power or high office.

The Torture Program

We will present you, the readers who comprise the jury, with overwhelming evidence that the defendants have committed and are responsible for heinous war crimes. Torture committed during a time of war is a war crime. The torture revealed in the photographs at Abu Ghraib, sadly, is illustrative of only a small part of a torture program implemented by the defendants after 9/11. It was a torture program that took place throughout the world, in Afghanistan, Iraq, Guantánamo, secret CIA prisons, and other places unknown.

Sadly, that torture program has not ended, and the Bush administration insists it will and must continue to use torture. It has fashioned laws so it can continue the torture program. In September 2006 President Bush, while claiming that he had not authorized torture, insisted that his administration could still employ an "alternative set of procedures" when prisoners stopped talking. These include torture and inhuman techniques such as sleep deprivation, stress positions including standing for long periods of time, raising and lowering of temperatures, and even the classic torture of waterboarding. Waterboarding is a medieval torture technique in which water is poured over and into the nose and mouth of victims to make them feel as if they are drowning. Evidence that this torture technique continues was revealed by the *New York Times*, which published information demonstrating that even after the administration publicly repudiated torture, it secretly issued opinions condoning waterboarding and other supposedly banned techniques. Evidence also comes from an unindicted co-conspirator, Vice President Dick Cheney, who in October 2006 admitted that he had no problem with waterboarding. A television reporter asked, "Would you agree a dunk in water is a no-brainer if it can save lives?" Cheney responded, "Well, it's a no-brainer for me." As the evidence will demonstrate, Cheney was one of the key architects of the torture program.

I want to say a word about the defendants in this case, those charged and those who are not. For now I will just give you their names, but you will hear more about each as we continue with this trial. Defendants include:

- Former Secretary of Defense Donald Rumsfeld
- Former CIA Director George Tenet
- Undersecretary of Defense for Intelligence Dr. Stephen Cambone
- Lieutenant General Ricardo Sanchez
- Major General Geoffrey Miller
- Major General Walter Wojdakowski
- Colonel Thomas Pappas
- Major General Barbara Fast
- Colonel Marc Warren
- Former Chief White House Counsel Alberto Gonzales
- General Counsel of the Department of Defense William James Haynes II
- Vice President Chief Counsel David Addington
- Former Deputy Assistant Attorney General John C. Yoo
- Former Assistant Attorney General Jay Bybee

You may have noticed that the two highest officials in the Bush administration, President Bush and Vice President Cheney, have not been named as defendants. This is not because of a lack of evidence against them. Both officials, in their public statements and in their private actions, have demonstrated their direct responsibility for the torture program. Some of the evidence against both of them is secret, but we know enough to demonstrate that they were instrumental in approving the torture program. We know, for example, that President Bush approved the non-application of the Geneva Convention to alleged terrorists—that eliminated a key legal restriction on torture; we know he signed an order that said detainees were to be treated humanely unless military necessity required otherwise—in other words, torture them if you need to; and we know he lied to the American people when he said, "We do not torture." We know that Cheney was one of the architects of the torture program and that he approved using "any means at our disposal" for dealing with alleged terrorists. Despite this, they cannot yet be defendants in this case, as Bush is the head of state and Cheney is the successor head of state; as such, they have immunity from criminal indictment while they are in office for acts that occurred during their tenure. The moment their terms are over, they can join the others as defendants. However, in this trial they have been named as unindicted co-conspirators for their role in the conspiracy to commit torture.

As you may also have noticed, some of the defendants in this case are attorneys. It is these attorneys—Alberto Gonzales, John Yoo, James Bybee, David Addington, and William Haynes—who provided the legal basis for much of the torture and abuse that occurred at Guantánamo, Abu Ghraib, and other U.S. detention facilities around the globe. While they may claim merely to have given legal opinions, those opinions were given in a context in which these defendants knew that torture would be the result of their fallacious legal reasoning. Without these opinions, the torture program would not have occurred. Lawyers can be liable criminally if they knowingly give unwarranted and false legal advice in situations where it is foreseeable that death or serious harm to people will result from that advice. Under this standard, there is sufficient evidence against the lawyer defendants in this case to warrant their conviction.

You may also ask, if these attorneys are defendants in this case, why isn't former Attorney General John Ashcroft listed as a defendant, even though he was in office during the time that the torture program was crafted? We fully expect evidence to come to light that will show without a doubt that President Bush, Vice President Cheney, and John Ashcroft were intimately involved in the creation of the torture program.

And this evidence is already beginning to come to light: according to an ABC News story from April 2008, Donald Rumsfeld, Dick Cheney, Colin Powell, Condoleezza Rice, George Tenet, and John Ashcroft held dozens of secret meetings to discuss the torture of detainees held in CIA custody. In these secret meetings, they apparently provided explicit approval of specific techniques to be used on individual detainees, including waterboarding, as well as the use of abusive interrogation techniques in combination.

Any torture is by definition barbaric. The Bush administration developed and implemented a scientific torture program, one that maximized the destruction of the human personality. You will be shocked, as the world has been, by what you see and what you read about this torture program. Human beings were stripped, hung from ceilings, beaten, threatened and attacked by dogs, sexually abused, subjected to hot and cold temperatures, deprived of food and sleep, waterboarded, and held in isolation day after day, month after month. More than occasionally, they died from torture.

This torture was not carried out by just a few "bad apples" as the defendants would have you believe. It was policy and practice ordered and approved at the highest levels of the Bush administration by the defendants listed earlier. The defendants have attempted to divert attention from their own actions by prosecuting low-level soldiers, particularly those photographed in the torture photos. But those pictures of torture were only the tip of the iceberg. The torture program was massive and ordered from the very top—from the Pentagon, from the CIA, and from the White House. To date no one high up in the chain of command, no one above the rank of Lt. Colonel has been prosecuted—and that officer, Steven Jordan, was not found guilty of any charges relating to torture. That is why we are here at this trial. We, the public, are the court of last resort. Our opinion perhaps can force some existing court somewhere to bring high-level officials of the Bush administration, the perpetrators of torture, to justice.

The Bush administration has made efforts, through public statements and publicly released memos, to mount a defense against the serious accusations of torture made against it. We will present you with their defenses and let you judge their adequacy. The Bush administration has argued from both sides of its mouth in its efforts simultaneously to deny that it has engaged in a torture program and to justify the use of torture. On the one hand, it claims it does not torture and treats prisoners humanely. As you will see, it makes this claim because it has redefined torture and inhuman treatment so that the coercive interrogations it employs do not come within what courts, treaties, and lawyers always found constituted torture. At the same time that it denies employing torture, the Bush administration insists that it needs harsh interrogation tactics to get information, and that the president, in the name of national security and self-defense, may employ torture. In fact, his lawyers argue that there are no limits on the cruelties he can impose on others if he thinks he needs to do so to make us safer. It will be for you to decide whether or not the Bush administration has engaged in torture, and it will be for you to decide whom among the administration to hold responsible.

The evidence will refute each of these so-called torture defenses. The Bush administration's assertion that it is not bound by any law is simply false. Democracies are built on certain principles, and the key principle is that authority of the executive is under law and not above law. Authority that operates above law is a dictatorship. We saw the principle that authority must adhere to law violated in Germany during the Nazi regime when the only law was what Hitler said the law was—it was called Führer's Law. The principle that authority is under law goes back at least to the Magna Carta of 1215 and is embodied in the core principles of the U.S. Constitution.

Nor is the claimed defense that torture can be employed in self-defense valid. Torture is immoral and illegal no matter the claimed necessity. In this prosecution of administration officials, we hesitate to argue that torture does not work. It does not, but we hesitate because we do not believe there are any circumstances that justify torture. Torture is a moral and legal issue, not a practical one.

Our experience has been that tortured people say whatever they can to stop the torture, and often the information is false. We think most of you know that torture is wrong, illegal, and immoral. However, many people in the United States either do not want to acknowledge that this is a country of torture or, out of fear of another terrorist attack, are willing tacitly to accept torture as necessary to make us safer. The Bush administration has played on this fear as a means of justifying its violations of fundamental rights including the prohibition against torture. But torture does not make us safer. It angers those who are tortured, and it angers people throughout the world. In the post-9/11 world, torture of Muslims at Abu Ghraib and Guantánamo angers Muslims who might otherwise be sympathetic to the United States. Imagine if it were Jews or Christians being tortured—would not people of those religions be angry? And that anger directed at the United States does not make us safer.

You might say, well, if torture does not work and it angers Muslims who might then attack us, why does the United States torture? Defendants claim that they need to get information and get it quickly in order to stop the next terrorist attack, and that torture helps them do so. This would still not make torture legal, but it would make the defendants appear more reasonable. The defendants say torture works and is necessary. Yet, history has shown the inefficiency of torture. The Gestapo used it in later years, but the results were completely unsuccessful. Many military officers and law enforcement officials, including senior members of the FBI, argue persuasively that torture does not work. The tortured person will say whatever is necessary to get the torture to stop, and rarely is the information true: the CIA's own Human Resource

Exploitation Manual of 1983 stresses that the use of force only induces the victim to say what he or she thinks the torturer wants to hear. An FBI interrogation instructor—Joe Navarro—stated in a December 2004 internal memo that, "the only thing that torture guarantees is pain, it never guarantees the truth."[1] Other FBI agents have also said torture doesn't work.[2] These officials say that softer, less coercive methods obtain information that is far superior. The evidence is strong that they are correct.

I do not know what was and is in the minds of the defendants and why, if torture does not work, they continue to insist on its use. Vengeance may be one motive. Another may be that the Bush administration wants to send its own message of terror to the Muslim world, wants to threaten those who might think about opposing U.S. policies with the terror of torture and imprisonment at places like Guantánamo. However, no matter the motives of the defendants, torture remains illegal and a violation of fundamental human rights.

In the next few pages I will outline the torture program of the Bush administration. This will give you an overview of the evidence. We will follow this brief introduction with undeniable proof, much of it from documents written by the defendants themselves, that these crimes were not committed by a few "bad apples" but were integral to a policy and practice authored and approved at the highest levels of the Bush administration. Its direct victims are in the thousands. Its indirect victims are all of us who care about morality, a government under law, and our own safety.

The Law

We begin with the law: the basic prohibition against torture and cruel, inhuman, and degrading treatment. These prohibitions are reflected in various treaties and statutes that were and are binding on the defendants. These include the Convention Against Torture, the Geneva Conventions, the War Crimes Statute and the Torture Statute. U.S. statutes provide long prison sentences and even the death penalty for those who torture. Torture, when committed during a war, is a war crime. These laws prohibit torture in any circumstances, by anyone—even if ordered or committed by a head of state. Nothing justifies torture. These laws, as well as legal precedents, also define torture and the types of treatment that are prohibited. The Convention Against Torture defines torture as "any act by which severe pain or suffering, whether physical or mental, is intentionally inflicted on a person for such purposes as obtaining from him or a third person information or a confession." International law, such as the Geneva Conventions, also prohibits less severe physical or mental pain. *Any form of physical treatment used to coerce someone during an interrogation is illegal.* When you read the evidence you will know that the Bush administration has engaged in torture and violated fundamental laws.

Torture and war crimes are considered so serious by the international community that they constitute an international crime that can be prosecuted and punished, irrespective of where, by whom, or against whom the act was committed. For such international crimes, the principle of universal jurisdiction applies—they can be prosecuted by any country. As you familiarize yourself with the evidence, keep in mind the seriousness of the universal prohibition against torture.

Systematic Torture

The first evidence we will present to you is example after example of the use of torture—the use of torture at Guantánamo, the use of torture at Abu Ghraib, and the use of torture at U.S. prisons and secret sites all over the world. Most of you will be aware of the photographs at Abu Ghraib, but torture was not limited just to that particular section of a certain prison in Iraq.

For example, the Center for Constitutional Rights represents Guantánamo detainee Mohammed al Qahtani in a case of torture in which the defendant, former Secretary of Defense Rumsfeld, was directly involved. The case was documented in a Guantánamo interrogation logbook for a period of 160 days. Al Qahtani was interrogated on 48 out of 160 days for eighteen to twenty hours a day. He was stripped, made to stand with spread legs in front of female guards, and mocked (so-called "invasion of space by a female"). He was forced to wear women's underwear on his head and to put on a bra, he was threatened by dogs and led on a leash, his mother was called a whore. In December 2002, al Qahtani was the target of a faked abduction and rendition. He was kept in the cold, given substances intravenously, not given access to a toilet, and deprived of sleep for weeks. At one point his heart rate fell to thirty-five beats per minute. In the case of al Qahtani, Rumsfeld and Major General Geoffrey Miller personally ordered practices that aimed to keep al Qahtani awake more than twenty hours per day for at least two months; probably longer.

CCR also represented former Guantánamo detainees called the Tipton Three. When I traveled to England, they told me their story. They said, "Well, we were picked up by one of the Northern Alliance war lords in Afghanistan, put into one of those shipping containers, and eventually sold to the Americans." They said, "We were assumed guilty when we went to Guantánamo." The interrogators showed them a picture of Osama bin Laden in a field with forty bearded Muslim men. And they said, "Isn't that you, and isn't that you in the picture?" And our clients said, "No, no, that's not us; we never met Osama; we never went to the al Farooq Training Camp. It's not us; we were working in Curry's in the U.K. at that time." But they were assumed guilty.

Then they told me about something I didn't know: the United States torture program. The men were put into small rooms and locked to a big metal bolt in the center of the floor. The temperature was taken up and down, they were stripped, they were hooded, they were sexually harassed, and then the interrogators would bring a dog in. American soldiers did all of this, including sleep deprivation, for a period of about ninety days to these men. This was standard at Guantánamo at this time. We didn't know it then, in March 2004. And I have to tell you, I was sitting there, and I sort of doubted some of their story. I said to myself, "Well, you know, maybe they're just exaggerating." This is before the photos of Abu Ghraib became public on April 28, 2004.

They told me that after being tortured, they made a false confession. They said that it *was* them in the photograph, even though it wasn't, and they said, "Yes, we knew Osama; we were trained in the al Farooq Training Camp."

Their story, or "confession," was completely false. But the details of their torture were not. Subsequently, the now famous Rumsfeld interrogation techniques were revealed, and the coercive torture methods used on the Tipton Three were outlined step by step in Rumsfeld's memo, which you can see in Chapter 3. On December 2, 2002, Rumsfeld signed the memorandum that allowed these techniques, including hooding, stripping, dogs, and sleep deprivation. At the end of this memorandum there is a note handwritten by Rumsfeld, which referred to the fact that prisoners were left standing in stress positions for up to four hours. In the note he wrote: "I stand 8 to 10 hours a day. Why is it limited to 4 hours?"

These are just some examples of the torture and inhuman treatment revealed by the evidence. They are by no means unique; nor do they reflect the worst of the treatment. There are literally thousands of cases of such torture. As you will discover, these tortures did not happen by chance, they did not happen because of the fog of war, and they did not happen because of a few rogue soldiers. The torture of these human beings was authorized and directed from the very highest levels of the U.S. government, by the very defendants that are before you.

Going to the Dark Side: The Case Against the Defendants

In the next few pages, I will give you a brief overview of evidence regarding the defendants' responsibility for the torture program. The defendants did not hide their plans, and they gave us warnings. For example, shortly after 9/11, Vice President Cheney practically acknowledged that unlawful methods would be employed. In an interview on national television, he stated: "We have to work the dark side, if you will." Beyond public statements of their intentions, their memoranda, orders, and actions deeply implicate the defendants in the authorization of torture.

Some of the first evidence we have of the defendants' culpability comes from early 2002. On January 19, 2002, defendant Rumsfeld informed the chief of the U.S. military, Richard B. Myers, that those detained in the war against Afghanistan would not be granted prisoner-of-war status as would normally be required by the Geneva Conventions. They would not even be given hearings to determine if they were prisoners of war. The government would "for the most part, treat them in a manner that is reasonably consistent with the Geneva Conventions to the extent appropriate."[3] With these few words, defendant Rumsfeld bypassed the humane protections of the Geneva Conventions and opened the door to torture.

This Rumsfeld memo was followed by an extraordinary memo written on January 25, 2002, by defendant Gonzales. In his memo Gonzales supported Rumsfeld and told the president why the United States should not follow the Geneva Conventions. A day later Secretary of State Colin Powell followed with a rebuttal. In his own memo Powell said that for the United States not to apply Geneva would undercut America's moral authority in the world and would endanger our soldiers. He argued that the United States was a pioneer in the development of the Conventions. In fact, the laws proscribing inhuman treatment came out of our own Civil War and were written to protect rights of all people. Powell argued that accepting Gonzales's memo would mean abandoning fundamental moral and legal principles.

Gonzales won the day. His memorandum paved the road to Abu Ghraib. He said that we had to interrogate people for intelligence, we had to give them summary trials, and Geneva's provisions on interrogation were obsolete, because while they allow you to interrogate people, they don't allow you to treat people inhumanly or to torture them. Gonzales noted that the War Crimes statute, a special criminal statute in the United States, prohibits violations of the Geneva Conventions. So he said to the president, in effect, "Look, the definition of 'inhuman' is vague, some prosecutor may come along in the future and decide that the way we're treating people is inhuman, and therefore we might be prosecuted, and the best way to avoid prosecution is simply to say the Geneva Conventions don't apply. If they don't apply, we can't violate them."

So what Gonzales really said in his memo was that yes, we are going to be treating people inhumanly, contrary to Geneva, and we must cover ourselves legally for the torture and inhuman treatment we are planning to inflict on prisoners. The president agreed with this memo and on February 7, 2002, issued a public statement denying prisoner-of-war status for the Taliban and any Geneva Conventions protection to alleged terrorists. He said all detainees should be treated humanely—but, and it is a big but— only "to the extent military necessity required." In other words, if torture was "necessary," it was permissible. The consequences of this stance would prove to be fatal.

Defendant Gonzales, with a push from Cheney and defendant Addington, asked for more memos to help make his argument that torture was legal; the most famous was called the Bybee/Yoo memo. That memorandum redefined torture so narrowly that classic and age-old tortures such as waterboarding were authorized to be employed and were subsequently employed by U.S.

officials. That memo would also be used to immunize those who tortured.

Defendant Bybee is now a federal judge in the Ninth Circuit, one of the most important circuits in the country, having been elevated to that job by the Bush administration. In the memo he wrote with John Yoo, dated August 1, 2002, Bybee made at least two sharp departures from legality. First, he took what I call the Pinochet defense. Pinochet, you all remember, tortured and murdered at least three thousand people in Chile in the name of national security. Defendant Bybee basically said (and I am paraphrasing here), "Look, in the name of national security, the president is exempt from laws prohibiting torture. He can do whatever he wants in the name of national security. The fact that we're signatories to and have ratified the Convention Against Torture, which makes it a crime, the fact that we have a criminal law that makes it a crime to torture people in the United States or outside the United States, the fact that it's customary international law not to torture, the fact that the Eighth Amendment to the Constitution essentially prohibits torture—none of that matters, because the president can do whatever he wants in the name of national security. And if the president can authorize torture, he can authorize those under him to torture, and that will be a defense to a criminal prosecution of all torturers."

Defendant Bybee also declared that torture is not torture. He redefined torture very narrowly so that almost any coercive interrogation technique would not constitute torture. Interrogators could do what they wanted to detainees. Therefore, taking a growling dog up to a naked man and saying, "It's going to bite your genitals off"—today that's not torture according to the Bybee/Yoo memo. Hanging someone from his or her wrists is not torture. Bybee and Yoo said in roughly these words that "Only physical pain that leads to organ failure or death is torture." Under that definition, almost none of what was seen in the pictures at Abu Ghraib constituted torture. In his testimony at his confirmation hearing for attorney general, Gonzales acknowledged that he had agreed with the conclusions of the Bybee memo. It was only three years later, at that hearing in January 2005, that Gonzales said the Bush administration now rejects that narrow definition and has gone back to one that the world accepts: torture is torture—intentionally inflicting significant pain, or putting someone in fear of serious physical injury is torture. So for over two-and-a-half years, under a definition of torture that essentially allowed everything short of murder, detainees around the world were tortured. Even today, Gonzales and the Bush administration hold to their view that non-citizens held outside the United States can be treated inhumanly and that neither the Geneva Conventions nor the prohibition on cruel, inhuman, and degrading treatment in the Convention Against Torture protects them. Their argument for this outrage is devoid of any legal merit.

After the Gonzales and the Bybee memos, we have the authorization for mistreatment and torture written by defendant Donald Rumsfeld. Did Rumsfeld know in advance about American soldiers piling naked prisoners in a heap in Abu Ghraib? I can't say for sure. But did his policy—the memos he authorized that said we don't have to pay attention to the Geneva Conventions, that we can use dogs against people, that we can use extreme interrogation techniques, that we can treat people inhumanly—did those memos and authorizations lead to Abu Ghraib? Absolutely. Did Rumsfeld authorize conduct that constituted war crimes? Absolutely.

The United States-led invasion of Iraq in the spring of 2003 led to the question of how the prisoners of war and so-called "illegal fighters" should be treated. This is when torture techniques started to be exported from Guantánamo to Iraq and used in the military prison of Abu Ghraib and other detention centers. This export was accomplished through a series of memoranda and instructions, in whose production and implementation, according to the report of the government's Schlesinger investigation, the entire military chain of command was involved.

In the wake of Abu Ghraib and the exposure of the torture memos, the Bush administration claims that it was not responsible for torture and inhuman treatment. The administration blames these behaviors on a "few bad apples" in Iraq and Afghanistan who chained some detainees to a ceiling and beat the heck out of them or sexually abused them, holding that those bad apples are responsible for excesses. But complicity in torture goes all the way up the chain of command, from Lt. General Sanchez in Iraq and General Miller, who was in Guantánamo and then traveled to Iraq, up to Secretary of Defense Rumsfeld, and finally to the President of the United States.

Upholding the laws prohibiting torture means acting against its propagation and insisting on the punishment of those directly responsible for torture as well as those who organize the practice of torture. This is the context in which the accusations in this trial should be understood. None of the defendants fulfilled their legally mandated roles to prohibit torture; all were complicit in the propagation of torture.

Continuing impunity for those who pulled the strings that led to the war crimes committed at Abu Ghraib and elsewhere is not acceptable. Condoning American torture emboldens other governments of the world to continue what is unfortunately their all-too-common practice of torture. It is precisely this situation that the U.S. Chief Prosecutor at the Nuremberg Trial, Robert Jackson, had in mind when he said this in his opening speech on November 21, 1945:

> Let me make clear that while this law is first applied against German aggressors, the law, if it is to serve a useful purpose, must condemn aggression by any other nations, including those which sit here now in judgment. We are able to do away with domestic tyranny and violence and aggression by those in power against the rights of their own people only when we make all men answerable to the law.

American torturers should not go unpunished.

2

Summary of the Indictment

I. Charges of War Crimes, Torture, and Other Forms of Cruel, Inhuman, or Degrading Treatment

The right of every human being to be free from torture and cruel, inhuman, or degrading treatment is universal and absolute. Under the laws of war, commission of such acts constitutes war crimes. War crimes and acts of torture are some of the most serious international crimes that exist. They are an attack on humanity as a whole, and it is in the interest of all that the authors of these crimes be prosecuted. For these reasons, international law provides that all states have an obligation to prosecute the alleged perpetrators of these crimes or turn them over to another state for prosecution. This obligation, first stated in the Geneva Conventions (Geneva III, art. 129; Geneva IV, art. 146), applies regardless of the nationality of the perpetrator, the nationality of the victim, or the place where the crime was committed, and applies regardless of the rank or political station of the perpetrator up to and including heads of state. This is the principle of universal jurisdiction, reaffirmed in the preamble of the Rome Statute of the International Criminal Court to which, in 2007, 104 countries are State Parties (but not the United States); universal jurisdiction is a principle now enacted by many states in their legislation.

Pursuant to international humanitarian law contained in the four Geneva Conventions of 1949,[1] ratified by the United States; pursuant to international human rights law under the International Covenant on Civil and Political Rights (ICCPR, arts. 7 & 10) and the Convention Against Torture and Other Cruel, Inhuman or Degrading Treatment or Punishment (Convention Against Torture), both of which are ratified by the United States; pursuant to the principles of customary international law applicable to all states; pursuant to the U.S. War Crimes Act of 1996 (18 U.S.C. § 2441) and to the Torture Victims Protection Act of 1994 (18 U.S.C. § 2340A), the following named individuals—**Donald Rumsfeld, George Tenet, Stephen Cambone, Ricardo Sanchez, Geoffrey Miller, Walter Wojdakowski, Thomas Pappas, Barbara Fast, Marc Warren, Alberto Gonzales, William Haynes, David Addington, John Yoo, and Jay Bybee**—are accused as guilty of war crimes and torture, and other cruel, inhuman, or degrading treatment.

II. Statement of the Offense

Hundreds of individuals were victims of gruesome crimes under international and American law, not only at the infamous Abu Ghraib prison, but in other U.S. detention centers in Iraq, Afghanistan, and Guantánamo Bay. The detainees' dignity—a natural and inalienable right possessed by all human beings—was taken from them. They were severely beaten, excessively deprived of sleep and food, sexually abused, raped or sodomized, sexually or religiously humiliated, stripped naked and hooded, and exposed to extreme temperatures and extreme noise. Some were killed, waterboarded, psychologically tortured, secretly detained, or rendered to a third country for torture. These acts consist of torture; cruel, inhuman, or degrading treatment; and war crimes.

III. The Defendants' Personal Responsibility

It is well established under international law and also under American law that individual criminal responsibility is not limited to persons who have directly perpetrated a crime. An individual is equally responsible for ordering, soliciting, aiding, or abetting a crime, and also responsible if he or she failed, as a civilian superior or as a military commander, to prevent its commission by subordinates, or failed to punish them.

Since September 11, 2001, and in the context of the so-called "war on terror," from Donald Rumsfeld on down, these political and military leaders have been personally in charge of ordering, implementing, and supervising the execution by lower-level soldiers of "harsh" interrogation techniques. These techniques were systematically used against hundreds of detainees in U.S. custody in Iraq, Afghanistan, and in the Guantánamo Bay prison camp. There is undeniable evidence, as we will show, that 1) these techniques amount to torture and/or cruel, inhuman, or degrading treatment, 2) in the context of an international armed conflict they also constitute war crimes, and 3) American military and civilian high-ranking officials are personally responsible for these crimes.

The defendants will deny personal responsibility or even knowledge, but we will show how their personal liability and knowledge has now been stated in a wide variety of official and nonofficial documents made public over the past few years. Following are summaries of the charges against each of them.

We begin with Department of Defense and high-ranking military officials, going all the way down the chain of command. We conclude with the legal architects of the Bush administration's torture program.

1. Donald Rumsfeld

Donald Rumsfeld was Secretary of Defense from 2001 until he resigned in November 2006. He is liable as a civilian commander over the military for his control over individuals accused of war crimes in Afghanistan, Guantánamo, and Iraq. In his position he was ultimately responsible for military policy. Former Secretary Rumsfeld was authorized by presidential military order to "detain individuals under such conditions [as] he may prescribe and to issue related orders and regulations as necessary."[2] Accordingly, Rumsfeld directed Department of Defense General Counsel, William Haynes, to establish a working group to study interrogation techniques. The working group played a significant role in relaxing the definition of torture, enabling Rumsfeld to authorize techniques viewed as impermissible by both military manuals and international law.

Donald Rumsfeld was directly responsible for war crimes. The severest abuses at Abu Ghraib occurred in the immediate aftermath of a decision by Rumsfeld to step up the hunt for "actionable intelligence" among Iraqi prisoners.

Former Secretary Rumsfeld approved a program for the use of force in interrogations, originally a Special Access Program (SAPs) for al Qaeda suspects, but also for use against numerous persons rounded up as detainees in Iraq. As Bart Gelman reported in the *Washington Post* in January 2005, Rumsfeld concluded that such operations need not be disclosed to Congress.

Two applicable directives of the Department of Defense (DOD), Directives 2310.1 and 5100.77, require that the U.S. military services comply with the principles, spirit, and intent of international laws of war; that the DOD observe and enforce the U.S. obligations under the laws of war; that personnel know the laws of war obligations; and that personnel promptly report incidents violating the laws of war and that the incidents be thoroughly investigated.

The interrogation training in use under the Bush administration is certainly inadequate when considered in light of these directives. The Army Field Manual 34-52 (FM 34-52), with its list of seventeen authorized interrogation methods, has long been the standard source of interrogation doctrine within the DOD. With a December 2, 2002, decision, Donald Rumsfeld authorized the use of sixteen additional techniques at Guantánamo, tactics ordinarily forbidden by the Army Field Manual. In April 2003, former Secretary Rumsfeld approved a list of about twenty interrogation techniques for use at Guantánamo Bay, that remain in force today; the techniques permit, among other things, reversing the normal sleep patterns of detainees and exposing them to heat, cold, and "sensory assault," including loud music and bright lights, according to defense officials. Documents exist proving that Rumsfeld directly and specifically approved such treatment for Guantánamo detainee Mohammed al Qahtani.

As Secretary of Defense, Rumsfeld was the penultimate civilian commander over the military, after President Bush. There is no doubt Rumsfeld had control over the individuals who committed war crimes; indeed, he ordered the commission of some war crimes, and set the conditions for the commission of others. Additionally, Rumsfeld failed to take appropriate action such as reporting and punishing when he first learned of the abuses, allowing the crimes to continue.

General Antonio Taguba, who investigated Abu Ghraib, submitted over a dozen copies of his report through channels at the Pentagon and the Central Command headquarters, and spent weeks briefing senior military leaders, said Rumsfeld was in public denial of the abuse up until the night of his Congressional testimony.

2. George Tenet

George Tenet became Acting Director of the Central Intelligence Agency (CIA) of the United States in 1996, and assumed the position of director in 1997, where he remained until his resignation in June 2004. As the director, Tenet had ultimate authority over all of the doings of the CIA and over all of its employees.

Tenet is responsible for war crimes when he personally solicited the detention of a "ghost detainee"—referring to people who are kept in CIA secret detention—and authorized programs in which CIA agents would unlawfully imprison, forcibly transfer, and torture people. As a result of the coercive techniques applied by the CIA under Tenet's leadership, numerous detainees in CIA custody have been killed during interrogation. Under Tenet's direction, the CIA also conducted false flag operations—hanging the flag of another country in the interrogation room in order to deceive the captive into thinking that he is imprisoned in a country with a reputation for brutality—a form of psychological torture prohibited by international law.

George Tenet failed to supervise those under his command where he had knowledge that war crimes and acts of torture were committed by his subordinates, and he did nothing to prevent those crimes.

Additionally, Tenet and the CIA failed to comply with requests to produce documentation for the various investigations conducted by the International Committee of the Red Cross (ICRC) and by the Department of Defense. While Tenet has instituted investigations into some of the deaths of those in custody, those investigations have occurred far too late, long after Tenet first had sufficient awareness of the CIA's illegal interrogation techniques. Tenet also ordered a general investigation into the CIA's interrogation techniques, but this order in May 2004 also came years after Tenet's knowledge of abuses by CIA agents.

3. Dr. Stephen Cambone

Dr. Stephen Cambone was the Undersecretary of Defense for Intelligence from 2003 until 2006. This position was created by

Secretary of Defense Donald Rumsfeld in his restructuring of the DOD. Cambone reported directly to Secretary Rumsfeld and was responsible for DOD intelligence activities. His official duties included coordinating DOD intelligence and intelligence-related policy, such as plans, resource allocations, and overseeing provision of intelligence support.

There is evidence that Cambone played a central role in the creation of secret interrogation operations. When the abuse of Iraqi prisoners at Abu Ghraib was revealed, Cambone was central to the bureaucratic chain of command that oversaw the interrogations. As Jason Vest reported in *The Nation*, the interrogations "were part of a highly classified Special Access Program (SAP) code-named Copper Green, authorized by Defense Secretary Donald Rumsfeld and ultimately overseen by Under Secretary of Defense for Intelligence Stephen Cambone."[3] Seymour Hersh revealed in an article in *The New Yorker* that while Copper Green had started out in Afghanistan using trained special operations personnel, in Iraq it involved using intelligence officers and other personnel not trained for the role.[4] After the CIA withdrew from the program, Cambone reportedly assigned Major General (MG) Miller, the former Guantánamo Bay interrogations chief, to oversee Iraq's prison system. It was after MG Miller's visit to Abu Ghraib that the most serious abuses occurred.

Cambone effectively had actual authority and control, as he was directly responsible to the Secretary of Defense for intelligence operations. Cambone had access to the Red Cross reports and the numerous complaints in the media about detainee conditions. Yet he failed in his duty to investigate further and failed to take action to halt impending war crimes.

4. Ricardo Sanchez

Ricardo Sanchez was a Lieutenant General (LTG) of the United States Army. After the fall of Baghdad in the spring of 2003, LTG

Sanchez assumed command of Combined Joint Task Force Seven (CJTF-7), which encompassed all U.S. armed forces in Iraq including those at all of the detention facilities. He held this position from June 14, 2003, until June 28, 2004.

Sanchez's September 14, 2003, authorization of certain interrogation procedures overstepped standard army doctrine and violated the Geneva Conventions' prohibition of inhuman treatment. The authorized methods included the use of military dogs, temperature extremes, yelling, loud music, light control, reversed sleep patterns, sensory deprivation, stress positions, prolonged isolation, and dietary manipulation. A month later, after Central Command of the Armed Forces had disapproved of the September techniques, LTG Sanchez issued an October 12, 2003, update of procedures that included "segregation" (or isolation) for extended periods and suggested that military dogs could still be used in interrogations.

The "Interrogation Rules of Engagement" were prominently posted in Abu Ghraib. The rules explicitly state that these methods could be used if the "CG's" (LTG Sanchez's) approval was sought and approved in writing. Sanchez himself acknowledged that "in twenty-five separate instances, he approved holding Iraqi prisoners in isolation for longer than thirty days, one of the methods listed in the posted rules."

LTG Sanchez knew of the abuses occurring at detention facilities under his command by late summer 2003 as a result of several reports, including the ICRC report. However, he did little, if anything, to stop those abuses or to implement the recommendations of these reports. LTG Sanchez retired on November 1, 2006.

5. Geoffrey Miller

Geoffrey Miller is a Major General with the United States Army. He was commander of Joint Task Force-Guantánamo (JTF-Guantánamo) from November 2002 until April 2004, when he became Deputy Commanding General of Detention Operations in Iraq, the position he held until July 31, 2006, when he resigned his post. As commander of JTF-Guantánamo, MG Miller oversaw both military intelligence and military police functions and had them work together to "soften up"[5] detainees for interrogation. In Iraq, Miller was responsible for all detainee operations, interrogation operations, and legal operations for multinational forces.

At MG Miller's direction, detainees at Guantánamo were held without contact with the outside world. Released detainees describe a range of treatments that individually and collectively amount to torture: being short-shackled in painful "stress positions" for many hours at a time, receiving deep flesh wounds and permanent scarring; being threatened by unmuzzled dogs; being forced to strip; being photographed naked; being subjected to repeated forced body cavity searches; being exposed to extremes of heat and cold for the purpose of causing suffering; being kept in filthy cages for twenty-four hours per day with no exercise or sanitation; being denied access to necessary medical care; being deprived of adequate food, sleep, communication with family and friends, and of information about their status; and being violently beaten by guards.

MG Miller was on notice of general abuses and the fact that conditions were ripe for abuse, yet he failed to take measures to ensure that abuses would not occur. As MG Miller encouraged the "softening up" of detainees, he authorized the abuses to take place, and when they did, he failed to take appropriate action by reporting these abuses to the proper authority. Miller has retired from duty as of July 31, 2006.

6. Walter Wojdakowski

Walter Wojdakowski is a U.S. Army Major General. He was the Deputy Commanding General (DCG) of the former CJTF-7 under Ricardo Sanchez. CJTF-7 encompassed all U.S. armed forces in

Iraq, including those deployed to detention facilities. MG Wojdakowski's CJTF-7 primary responsibility was to support such facilities. He also had direct responsibility and oversight of the separate brigades assigned to CJTF-7.

MG Wojdakowski directly authorized illegal interrogation techniques. The *Washington Post* revealed this fact in May 2004: "[Colonel Thomas] Pappas said, among other things, that interrogation plans involving the use of dogs, shackling, or similar aggressive measures followed [LTG] Sanchez's policy, but were often approved by Sanchez's deputy, Maj. Gen. Walter Wojdakowski, or by Pappas himself." MG Wojdakowski's approval of certain interrogation procedures contravened standard army doctrine and the Geneva Conventions' prohibitions of inhuman and degrading treatment.

As the DCG of CJTF-7 with direct responsibility over the 205th Military Intelligence (MI) Brigade and Colonel (COL) Pappas, MG Wojdakowski's general responsibility over all U.S. armed forces in Iraq and over commanders of these forces cannot be questioned.

Wojdakowski knew about the abuses as early as November 2003, and then failed to inform his immediate supervisor. The authors of the Schlesinger, Fay-Jones, and Taguba reports—all key investigations into the torture and abuse at Abu Ghraib—as well as congressional testimony, have underscored MG Wojdakowski's failure to provide proper guidance, supervision, and oversight of detention operations and staff. MG Wojdakowski is now Commanding General of Fort Benning.

7. Thomas Pappas

Thomas Pappas is a Colonel of the U.S. Army. Since July 1, 2003, he has been the Commander of the 205th MI Brigade deployed in Iraq. From November 19, 2003, until February 6, 2004, COL Pappas was designated by the CJFT-7 as the Commander for Force Protection and Security of Detainees of Forward Operating Base

(FOB) Abu Ghraib and thus took tactical control of the prison of Abu Ghraib during that time.

COL Pappas authorized and ordered the misuse of dogs to support interrogations to "fear up"[6] detainees. He said MG Miller told him dogs were acceptable for use in setting the atmosphere during interrogations. COL Pappas requested the use of navy dogs to intimidate the detainees. When an army investigator asked Pappas how intimidation with dogs could be allowed under existing treaties, Pappas gave the chilling reply, "I did not personally look at that with regard to the Geneva Convention."

Since COL Pappas had effective authority over Abu Ghraib, the 205th MI Brigade and therefore the 800th Military Police (MP) Brigade, he was responsible for his subordinates' acts. Evidence shows that not only did COL Pappas have knowledge of crimes committed by his subordinates, but that he was present when they occurred. COL Pappas told MG Taguba that intelligence officers sometimes instructed Military Police to strip detainees naked and to shackle them in preparation for interrogation when there was no good reason to do so. On November 4, 2003, Iraqi detainee al-Jamadi died at Abu Ghraib while being questioned by a CIA officer and Navy Seal soldiers, face down and handcuffed. The autopsy showed the death stemmed from a blood clot caused by injuries sustained during apprehension. According to Captain Donald Reese, COL Pappas was the senior officer present during the death.

The Taguba report stated that COL Pappas "[f]ailed to ensure that Soldiers under his direct command were properly trained in and followed the Interrogation Rules of Engagement; Failed to ensure that Soldiers under his direct command knew, understood, and followed the protections afforded to detainees in the Geneva Convention relative to the Treatment of Prisoners of War."

Pappas was punished only nonjudicially, not through a court-martial or other court proceeding. No substantive criminal charges have been brought against him. Pappas currently has the same job he had when the abuses at Abu Ghraib occurred: Commander of the 205th MI Brigade.

8. Barbara Fast

Barbara Fast is a Major General with the United States Army. She was a Senior Intelligence Officer with the CTJF-7 in Iraq and a member of the Detainee Release Board. She was a subordinate of LTG Sanchez, the Commander of the CTJF-7 and intermittently Pappas's superior.

Barbara Fast is alleged to have refrained from preventing war crimes from being committed by her subordinates, despite her authority to do so.

The Schlesinger Report explicitly points out that the CJTF-7 Commander 2, Barbara Fast, Director of Intelligence, failed to advise the commander (Sanchez) properly on directives and policies needed for the operations of the Joint Interrogation and Debriefing Center [JIDC]. The JIDC is the physical location for the exploitation of intelligence information from enemy prisoners of war. The JIDC may also interrogate civilian detainees, refugees, and other nonprisoner sources.

According to the report of 2004 by George R. Fay on Intelligence Activities at Abu Ghraib, Fast also inadequately monitored "the activities of Other Government Agencies" (CIA operations at the Abu Ghraib facility) "within the Joint Area Operations."

In her role as a chief military intelligence officer in Abu Ghraib, she then had actual and effective control over the ongoing incidents. In fact, although the soldiers who perpetrated the abuses in Abu Ghraib were not her direct subordinates, she still had the authority and control to prevent further crimes. She did not do so, yet no disciplinary action has been taken against her and no criminal investigation is contemplated.

Barbara Fast is currently the commanding General of the Army Intelligence Center at Fort Huachuca, where, disturbingly, troops learn interrogation methods and the army rules on the treatment of prisoners.

9. Marc Warren

Marc Warren is a Colonel with the United States Army. Under the command of LTG Ricardo Sanchez, in 2003-04, he was a staff judge advocate for the CJTF-7 and as such the highest legal expert within the U.S. military apparatus in Iraq. His assignment was to provide legal advice to General Sanchez on whether or not his orders and memoranda were pursuant to the Geneva Conventions.

Marc Warren mandated Captain Brent Fitch, Major Daniel Kazmier, and Major Franklin D. Raab to draft new reliable interrogation rules. Captain Fitch adopted the memorandum of the Secretary of Defense Donald Rumsfeld from April 16, 2003, "almost verbatim" and added proposals of the 519th Military Intelligence Battalion, which included some further abusive techniques such as the use of dogs, which he authorized for all detainees. This document was approved by Warren.

Sanchez trusted the advice of his Judge Advocate that he had the authority to enact a directive of aggressive interrogation methods as the Commander of the Combined Joint Task Force. Sanchez's decisions were grounded on Warren's legal advice.

After the first surprise visit to the Abu Ghraib prison of the ICRC in mid-October 2003 and its following report—which already included images of naked detainees and detainees in women's underwear—Warren claimed that neither he nor anyone else from CJTF-7 headquarters was present in Abu Ghraib when the Red Cross arrived for its investigations.

The Fay-Jones report documents that Warren and Wojdakowski attended a meeting in the beginning of December 2003 to debate the response to the ICRC report with the aim of invalidating its allegations. The Schlesinger report asserts that "[t]he CJTF-7 Staff Judge Advocate failed to initiate an appropriate response to the

November 2003 ICRC report on the conditions at Abu Ghraib." The reply letter to the ICRC was drafted by the office of Marc Warren, and was sent over with Warren's signature. Warren denied in his testimony before the Senate Armed Services Committee on May 19, 2004, that he had written the letter, but said he "believed" that others in his office did. The letter informs the Red Cross that the U.S. military need not fully apply the Geneva Conventions at Abu Ghraib.

10. Alberto Gonzales

Alberto Gonzales was commissioned as chief White House counsel (WHC) to President George W. Bush in January 2001, and remained in that position until he was sworn in as attorney general on February 3, 2005. As chief WHC, Gonzales was responsible for advising the president on all legal issues concerning the president and the White House. He was also responsible for coordinating communications between the White House and the Justice Department's Office of Legal Counsel (OLC). It is important to note that while many think the WHC is the president's personal counsel, the WHC is in fact employed by the American public and is meant to serve their interests, not the president's.

In this capacity, he presumably briefed the president on all of the major memoranda sent to the president on the applicability of the Geneva Conventions and the scope of the Convention Against Torture and the federal War Crimes Act.

In his own memorandum to the president of January 25, 2002, Gonzales endorsed legal opinions supporting extreme presidential authority to remove the protections afforded by these Conventions and also endorsed opinions that found the obligations under international treaties to be nonbinding. His advocacy of the withdrawal of Geneva protections was a necessary precursor to the creation of the legal black hole that allowed torture to take place.

Under the most basic standards of complicity in aiding and abetting torture and committing war crimes, Gonzales's activities make him personally criminally responsible for advocating for the removal of the protections guaranteed under the Geneva Conventions. His omissions—in the form of failing to object to arguments advanced by the subordinates—make him legally responsible for paving the way for violations of the Geneva Conventions and the Convention Against Torture, charges that constitute war crimes. As a consequence of Gonzales's actions, hundreds of detainees have been abused and tortured in U.S.-operated detention facilities.

Finally, in October 2007, it was revealed by the *New York Times* that a series of secret memos and legal opinions had been approved by Attorney General Gonzales in 2005, for the first time explicitly authorizing U.S. interrogators to use a combination of brutal interrogation techniques in tandem. The approved techniques include, for example, the use of extreme cold and head slapping, and, for the first time, waterboarding was explicitly authorized. These secret memos remain, today, the prevailing legal justifications for the ongoing torture of those held by the CIA.

11. William Haynes

Former General Counsel William Haynes was, beginning in May 2001, the direct legal advisor to former Secretary of Defense Donald Rumsfeld. Haynes was one of the architects and chief defenders of the Bush administration's illegal policies regarding detainee treatment. Haynes ignored domestic law as well as U.S. treaty obligations and established principles of international law when he recommended approval of interrogation techniques that amounted to cruel, inhuman, and degrading treatment. Haynes's blanket approval of illegal techniques gave the green light to U.S. servicemen to abuse and torture detainees in U.S. custody.

Haynes led a DOD working group that advocated circumventing

detainee treatment safeguards prescribed by U.S. domestic law, the Geneva Conventions, and longstanding U.S. military practice. In the face of serious legal criticism from career military attorneys, the working group approved interrogation techniques amounting to cruel, inhuman, and degrading treatment; limited the number of prohibited techniques by narrowly redefining torture; argued that the president has the authority to ignore U.S. law prohibiting torture and to immunize officials who violate the law; and claimed that U.S. law governing detainee treatment does not apply in Guantánamo Bay and other territories outside the United States. As a consequence of Haynes's actions, individuals not charged with any crime have been denied their most basic rights.

The legal opinion provided by General Counsel Haynes was legally derelict. At the same time, it is highly unlikely that Rumsfeld would or could have approved torture tactics without justification and approval from his top legal advisor. Had Haynes provided an accurate assessment of the state of the law instead of manipulating the law to arrive at his desired outcome, Rumsfeld most likely would not have authorized the interrogation tactics. Haynes's conduct constituted a "substantial effect" on Rumsfeld's approval of illegal interrogation methods.

There has been no disciplinary action taken against former General Counsel Haynes. President Bush nominated him to the U.S. Court of Appeals for the Fourth Circuit; because of strong opposition, Haynes withdrew from consideration. He resigned as General Counsel of the Department of Defense in February 2008.

12. David Addington

David Addington was Vice President Richard Cheney's chief of staff from December 28, 2000, until he was promoted in October 2005 to Chief Counsel. He reviews the statements of the vice president and advises on legal issues as they relate to policy. He also advises the staff about questions of ethics. The chief of staff is responsible for directing, managing, and overseeing all policy development, daily operations, and staff activities for the vice president.

A series of memoranda written in the first months after 9/11 by John Yoo of the Justice Department's OLC were allegedly heavily influenced by Addington.[7] The first, on September 25, 2001, claimed that the president was not bound by proscriptions on torture in international treaties or domestic statutes and "claim[ed] that there were virtually no valid legal prohibitions against the inhuman treatment of foreign prisoners held by the C.I.A. outside the U.S."[8] This conclusion is patently legally false.

Addington has consistently averred—in the face of massive precedents to the contrary—that under the constitution, the president has unlimited powers as commander-in-chief during wartime. Addington helped to shape an August 2002 opinion from the Justice Department's OLC that said torture might be justified in some cases. According to a government insider who was a part of early internal debates following 9/11, Addington accused those who favored compliance with international law of being "soft on terrorism."

13. John C. Yoo

John C. Yoo served as deputy assistant attorney general in the OLC within the Department of Justice from July 2001 through June 2003. As deputy assistant attorney general, Yoo worked under the OLC assistant attorney general, Jay S. Bybee.

Yoo's memos created the legal justification for torture and abuse of detainees held in the U.S. war on terror. His January 9, 2002, memo stripped away the floor of fundamental rights that the Geneva Conventions provide to both formal POWs and to "unlawful combatants," which is not a legal category, but a term coined by the Bush administration. By arguing that the Geneva Conventions did not apply in any way to these detainees and by failing to articulate any kind of minimal standard for detainee treatment outside of Geneva, Yoo provided a legal justification for interrogation methods that included torture and cruel, inhuman, or degrading treatment. His memorandum from August 2002 narrowed the definition of torture to acts that inflicted pain equivalent to major organ failure or death, effectively authorizing a range of interrogation methods commonly considered to be torture.

Yoo reasserted some of his most irresponsible, least-founded legal conclusions on torture and unbridled executive power in the April 2003 Working Group Report, which was used to justify several official interrogation techniques that constituted torture or cruel, inhuman, and degrading treatment. The total result of these legal opinions was the granting of legal cover to the systematic torture of detainees held in the so-called "war on terror."

As the author of these memoranda, Yoo aided and abetted war crimes under international law, and facilitated torture and cruel, inhuman, and degrading treatment of detainees in Guantánamo Bay, Afghanistan, and Iraq.

No disciplinary action has been taken against John Yoo. After leaving the OLC in 2003, Yoo returned to his tenured position as Professor of Law at Boalt Hall, University of California Berkeley.

14. Jay Bybee

Jay Bybee was the assistant attorney general for the OLC in the Justice Department from October 2001 until March 2003.

At the OLC, Bybee wrote memos outlining the Bush administration's legal framework for the war on terrorism. The most important memo is the August 1, 2002, so-called "torture memo," which examined a 1994 statute ratifying the United Nations Convention against Torture (CAT). To constitute torture under this convention, Bybee concluded, physical pain must be "equivalent in intensity to the pain accompanying serious physical injury, such as organ failure, impairment of bodily function, or even death." Moreover, inflicting that severe pain must have been the "specific intent" of the interrogator. Bybee also asserted that the U.S. ratification of the 1994 statute could be unconstitutional if it interfered with the president's commander-in-chief powers. Bybee incorrectly asserted that the CAT leaves cruel, inhuman, or degrading treatment "without the stigma of criminal penalties." Bybee nowhere mentions that cruel and degrading treatment is forbidden under the Fifth, Eighth, and Fourteenth Amendments of the U.S. Constitution, a serious dereliction of his legal duties.

The torture memo was used by the Bush administration as "sweeping legal authority" for harsh interrogations of foreign detainees and became national policy for twenty-two months until, after widespread criticism of the torture memo, the Justice Department rescinded it on December 30, 2004.

Bybee's actions satisfy the requirements of aiding and abetting liability. By writing the torture memo with knowledge that OLC's legal opinions carry great weight to the executive branch, and by keeping the memo secret from the public, Jay Bybee knowingly facilitated illegal abuses at Abu Ghraib and elsewhere.

Bybee is currently a federal judge for the 9th Circuit U.S. Court of Appeals.

3

Evidence for the Prosecution

In this chapter, you will read expert testimony as well as primary source documents from attorneys, U.S. interrogators who served in Iraq, detainees from Guantánamo Bay, as well as accounts of the abuse of Iraqi prisoners that prove the defendants engaged in a post-9/11 program of torture and abuse.

GUANTÁNAMO

Four months after 9/11, on January 11, 2002, the U.S. military flew twenty prisoners from Afghanistan to the U.S. naval base at Guantánamo Bay, Cuba. Hundreds would soon follow, as would allegations of torture and abuse, public outcry both at home and abroad over the mistreatment of detainees, and repeated calls for the closure of Guantánamo.

In the six years hence, the total number of detainees held at the base rose to almost 800—some as young as ten, others as old as eighty. As of April 2008, there remained approximately 280 men in detention, despite many of them having been cleared for release for years. Guantánamo has become a Kafkaesque symbol of the U.S. government's deeply flawed "war on terror," a place where the rule of law does not apply.

The following section includes testimony from former Guantánamo detainees on their torture and abuse while held at the prison camp; documents detailing the torture of prisoner Mohammed al Qahtani, including a government log that meticulously reports the specific interrogation methods used against him; and memos signed by Donald Rumsfeld authorizing specific interrogation tactics that amount to torture.

Tipton Three Report Excerpts

The following document consists of excerpts from a report assembled by the Center for Constitutional Rights, drawing on the first-hand accounts by three British citizens of the abuse and torture they experienced while they were in U.S. custody in Afghanistan and at Guantánamo.

The "Tipton Three"—Shafiq Rasul, Asif Iqbal, and Rhuhel Ahmed—were detained in northern Afghanistan on November 28, 2001. In March 2004, they were released from Guantánamo. CCR represented Mr. Rasul and Mr. Iqbal in Rasul v. Bush, *the historic Supreme Court case that successfully challenged the Bush administration's policy of indefinitely holding detainees at Guantánamo Bay without judicial review. The report was compiled as evidence in CCR's German case against Donald Rumsfeld.*

These excerpts focus on the experiences of Shafiq Rasul while detained at Guantánamo.

During the whole time that we were in Guantánamo, we were at a high level of fear. When we first got there the level was sky-high. At the beginning we were terrified that we might be killed at any minute. The guards would say to us "we could kill you at any time." They would say "the world doesn't know you're here, nobody knows you're here, all they know is that you're missing and we could kill you and no one would know."

After time passed, that level of fear came down somewhat but never vanished. It was always there. We were in a situation where there was no one we could complain to and not only could they do anything to any of us but we could see them doing it to other detainees. All the time we thought that we would never get out. Most especially if we were in isolation there would be a constant fear of what was happening and what was going to happen.

Isolation and Interrogations (May/August 2003)
After about a week I was in my cell when I heard a guard talking to a detainee in the cell next to me and saying "look at that

British guy next to you, we have found out that he and his two friends from Britain are terrorists and linked to Al-Qaeda as well. We have found videos which prove that they are linked to the men who carried out the September 11th attacks." When I heard this I called the soldier over and said "what is all this about?" He told me that "my superiors have told me that they have found video evidence on you and your two friends." I was extremely shocked and did not have a clue about what he was talking about. I didn't see that soldier again.

About a week later I was suddenly collected and taken to one of the three isolation blocks, "November." I asked the Sergeant why I was being moved and he simply said "we don't know. The order is from the interrogators." I was placed in a metal cell painted green inside. It was filthy and very rusty. There was a tap, sink, toilet and a metal bunk. It was extremely hot, hotter than the other cells I'd been in previously. Although there was an air conditioning unit it was turned off so the cells were much hotter than the ones I was previously held in because they were completely closed off and no air could come into the cell. There was a glass panel at the hatch at the front of the cell so they could keep an eye on us. Whilst it was extremely hot in the daytime, at night when it got cold, anyway, they would turn the air conditioning up so that it became freezing. I didn't have a blanket or a mattress and had only my clothes to keep me warm so I got absolutely freezing at night. For the first week I had no idea what was going on. I was not taken to interrogation; I just had to sit there waiting. I felt like I was going out of my mind. I didn't know where the others were, I didn't know why I was being held there. Nobody would talk to me. I was taken out maybe just twice for showers but that was it. I was extremely anxious. Then about a week later I was taken by two soldiers to interrogation at the Gold building.

I was taken into a room and short shackled. This was the first time this had happened to me. It was extremely uncomfortable.

Short shackling means that the hands and feet are shackled together forcing you to stay in an uncomfortable position for long hours. Then they turned the air conditioning on to extremely high so I started getting very cold. I was left in this position on my own in the room for about 6 or 7 hours, nobody came to see me. I wanted to use the toilet and called for the guards but nobody came for me. Being held in the short shackled position was extremely painful but if you tried to move the shackles would cut into your ankles or wrists. By the time that I was eventually released to be taken back to my cell I could hardly walk as my legs had gone completely numb. I also had severe back pains.

I was returned to my cell with no explanation as to why I had been brought to interrogation and I was then left in the Isolation cell for a further week. Again, nobody would explain to me what was going on and I felt I was going crazy inside my head. Some time during that week I saw Asif and Rhuhel being brought into the November block and placed in cells further down the corridor.

The next day after Asif and Rhuhel had arrived I was taken to interrogation in the Gold building. I was long shackled and chained to the floor. There was an interrogator in the room this time. He showed me some pictures which I later discovered were stills taken from a video. The pictures showed about 40 people sitting on the floor in a field. He asked me if I recognized anybody in the picture. The picture was not very clear and I didn't recognize anybody.

He then showed me another picture where three people were sitting together and there were arrows pointing with my name as well as Asif and Rhuhel's name. Behind the three men who were supposedly the three of us there was another person with an arrow indicating that he was Mohammed Atta one of the September 11th hijackers. I don't know whether the picture was

Mohammed Atta or not, the man in the photograph had a beard whereas the only pictures I've seen of Mohammed Atta are of him being clean shaven. I believe the interrogator was from Army Intelligence. He was an American Arabic guy who I knew by the name Bashir although other interrogators called him Danny. He started basically accusing me of being present at the meeting, of being the person in the picture and of being involved with Al-Qaeda and with September 11th hijackings. I was denying it but he wouldn't believe me.

When I saw the photographs I could see that they were purportedly from 2000 and I knew that I was in England during that time, which I told him.

After the first interrogation I was brought back to my cell and then a few days later brought out again. This time I was short shackled. I was left squatting for about an hour and then this Bashir came back again and he started questioning me again about the photographs and trying to get me to admit that I was in the photographs. I was telling him that if you check you will find out that I was in England during this time. After a while he left the room and I was left again in the short shackle position for several hours (I think for about 4 hours) before I was eventually taken back to the cells. When we were left in the interrogation rooms we were not provided with food and we missed meals. We also missed our prayers.

After this I was taken back to my cell and then at intervals of about 4 or 5 days at a time I was brought back to the same interrogation block where I was short shackled and left for hours at a time and not interrogated at all. This happened about 5 or 6 times.

On a couple of occasions when I was left in the short shackle position they would play extremely loud rock or heavy metal music which was deafening. Probably the longest period of time I was left in the short shackle position was 7 or 8 hours, which was on the first occasion. On other occasions I would be left in the room for up to 12 to 13 hours but in the long shackle position. Nobody would come in. Occasionally someone would come and say that an interrogator was on their way but they wouldn't turn up. For a period of about 3 weeks I was taken backwards and forwards to interrogation but not actually asked any questions.

Mohammed al Qahtani

The following two documents starkly illustrate the torture techniques author-ized by Donald Rumsfeld. The first is a declaration prepared by attorney Gi-tanjali Gutierrez based on first-hand accounts of Guantánamo detainee Mohammed al Qahtani provided to Gutierrez during her visits with him. Mr. al Qahtani's recounting of his experiences is supplemented by relevant informa-tion obtained by Gutierrez in the course of representing al Qahtani.

Mohammed al Qahtani is a Saudi Arabian man who was transferred to Guantánamo in January 2002. Once there, he was harshly interrogated through aggressive techniques specifically authorized by then-Secretary of Defense Donald Rumsfeld, known as the "First Special Interrogation Plan." These methods included, but were not limited to, forty-eight days of severe sleep deprivation and twenty-hour interrogations, forced nudity, sexual hu-miliation, religious humiliation, physical force, prolonged stress positions, prolonged sensory overstimulation, and threats with military dogs. The ag-gressive techniques alone and in combination, resulted in severe physical and mental pain and suffering. To this day, Mr. al Qahtani has not received any therapeutic medical evaluation of or treatment for the physical and psycho-logical injuries from his abuse. He continues to suffer from ongoing psycho-logical pain and suffering arising from his torture and cruel, inhuman, and degrading treatment. He continues to be held at Guantánamo. Al Qahtani's habeas petition was dismissed, and his attorneys then filed a Detainee Treat-ment Act petition in the D.C. Court of Appeals on his behalf. The government has also charged al Qahtani in the military commissions and plans to seek the death penalty against him. CCR will be assisting in his defense.

The declaration that follows was prepared and submitted by the Center for Constitutional Rights as part of the German complaint against Donald Rumsfeld.

The second document is an excerpt from a declassified military log that details forty-nine days of al Qahtani's twenty-hour-long interrogation ses-sions and the interrogation techniques that were used on him. Excerpted here are two days out of the forty-nine.

CCR Attorney Gitanjali Gutierrez on the Torture
of Guantánamo Detainee Mohammed al Qahtani

At some point in early September 2002, military intelligence personnel at Guantánamo began planning a new, more aggressive interrogation regime for Mr. al Qahtani. Military intelligence officials wanted to apply the training tactics used in the "SERE" program, the Survival, Evasion, Resistance and Escape training program for U.S. Special Forces. The SERE program is designed to teach U.S. soldiers how to resist torture techniques if they are captured by enemy forces. In Guantánamo, though, military intelligence officials wanted to use the training methods as interrogation techniques against Mr. al Qahtani and others. The SERE training program involves forms of torture such as religious and sexual humiliation, and waterboarding.

Major General Michael Dunlavey, the Commander of the Guantánamo detention center, sent a request up the chain of command on October 11, 2002 for approval for an interrogation plan for Mr. al Qahtani that included 19 techniques outside the traditional guidelines for military interrogations. These techniques included:

1. *Category I*: Yelling, deception, use of multiple interrogators, misrepresenting the identity of the interrogation (as if from a country with a reputation for harsh treatment of prisoners);

2. *Category II*: Stress positions (such as standing for up to four hours), use of falsified documents or reports, isolation for 30 days or longer, interrogation in places other than the interrogation booth, deprivation of light and sound, hooding, interrogation for up to 20 hours straight, removal of all comfort items (including religious items), switching from hot food to military meals ready to eat, removal of clothing, forced grooming and shaving of facial hair, use of phobias (such as fear of dogs) to induce stress; and

3. *Category III*: Uses of scenarios to persuade the detainee that death or pain is imminent for him or his family, exposures to cold or water, use of mild non-injurious physical contact, use of a wet towel or waterboarding to simulate drowning or suffocation.

Details of his interrogation regime, officially known as the "First Special Interrogation Plan," emerged when a military interrogation log for Mr. al Qahtani was leaked from Guantánamo. The log describes six weeks of physical and psychological interrogation methods that involved prolonged sleep deprivation; painful stress positions; physical abuses; sexual, physical, psychological and religious humiliation; the use of military dogs; and sensory overstimulation. According to some news accounts, Mr. al Qahtani endured at least 160 days of severe isolation in a cell constantly flooded with light, with much of this time also including interrogations using aggressive tactics as part of the First Special Interrogation Plan.

On December 2, 2002, Secretary Donald Rumsfeld personally approved 16 of the aggressive interrogation techniques for use against Mr. al Qahtani. The memorandum authorized techniques, used alone or in tandem, such as forced nudity; stress positions; religious humiliation (removal of religious items and forcible shaving of beards and hair); isolation of up to 30 days with extensions possible after command approval; light and sound deprivation: exploitation of phobias (such as fear of dogs); and "mild" physical contact. He also approved one tactic in Category III, "mild non-injurious physical contact."

Secretary Rumsfeld also secretly authorized 24 techniques in March 2003, including isolation, "environmental manipulation," "sleep adjustment," and threats to send the detainee to a country allowing torture. As a result of these authorizations for aggressive interrogation tactics, Mr. al Qahtani's abuse continued during 2003.

Torture and Abuse of Mohammed al Qahtani During Interrogations
An FBI Deputy Director reported to the army that in November 2002, he observed a detainee, later identified as Mr. al Qahtani, exhibiting symptoms of "extreme psychological trauma" that included talking to non-existent people, reportedly hearing voices, and crouching in a corner of the cell covered with a sheet for hours on end.[1]

In September 2006, Mr. al Qahtani described to me some of the methods used against him during interrogations in 2002 and 2003:

- Severe sleep deprivation combined with twenty-hour interrogations for months at a time
- Severe isolation
- Religious and sexual humiliation
- Threats of rendition to countries that torture more than the United States
- Threats made against his family, including female members of his family
- Strip searching, body searches, and forced nudity, including in the presence of female personnel
- Denial of the right to practice his religion, including prohibiting him from praying for prolonged times and during Ramadan
- Threatening to desecrate the Koran in front of him
- Placing him in stress positions for prolonged times
- Placing him in tight restraints repeatedly for many months or days and nights
- Threats and attacks by dogs
- Beatings

- Exposure to low temperatures for prolonged times
- Exposure to loud music for prolonged times
- Forcible administration of frequent IVs by medical personnel during interrogation, which Mr. al Qahtani described as feeling like "repetitive stabs" each day.

Some of these methods used against Mr. al Qahtani are described in detail below.

Sleep Deprivation

Mr. al Qahtani reported severe sleep deprivation, often being permitted only to sleep four or fewer hours at a time, over prolonged periods of time. U.S. military authorities imposed this sleep deprivation through the use of interrogations lasting twenty hours, shifting Mr. al Qahtani to a new cell throughout the night, imprisoning him in cells with twenty-four-hour lighting, altering his sleep patterns by only allowing him to sleep during the day, and by creating disruptive noise to wake him up. In order to facilitate twenty-hour interrogations, if Mr. al Qahtani began to fall asleep from exhaustion, military police or interrogators would forcibly make him stand and sit, pour water on him, or otherwise physically abuse him. They conducted one interrogation shift after another to keep the interrogators refreshed and active while Mr. al Qahtani continued to deteriorate from exhaustion.

Because Mr. al Qahtani's sleep deprivation was only one act in a course of torturous conduct, his sleep deprivation should also be considered in relation to other torturous acts occurring during his interrogation.

As a result of his torture, Mr. al Qahtani began hallucinating and hearing voices, urinated on himself multiple times, and frequently broke down into tears. Thus, his sleep deprivation, when considered in light of the intensity and duration of the overall course of conduct he was subjected to, constituted torture.

The defendants expressly authorized prolonged and severe sleep deprivation as an interrogation tactic for use against Mr. al Qahtani. Secretary Rumsfeld officially authorized the use of twenty-hour interrogations without limit in his December 2, 2002, memorandum. For at least two months, and likely for additional periods, military authorities under the command of Secretary Rumsfeld and General Miller authorized and implemented practices intended to keep Mr. al Qahtani awake for twenty hours per day for two months.

Severe Isolation Combined with Sensory Deprivation/Overstimulation
For 160 days within his first two years of imprisonment, military authorities held Mr. al Qahtani in severe isolation, in which he could not communicate with other detainees in any fashion.[2] Prior to meeting with me, Mr. al Qahtani was completely dependent on his interrogators for any information, including information concerning his family.

Secretary Rumsfeld and General Miller authorized, were aware of, and supervised Mr. al Qahtani's isolation and sensory deprivation. These were not single acts of misconduct by rogue individuals but rather an intentional and official aspect of Mr. al Qahtani's interrogation at Guantánamo.

Religious, Sexual, and Moral Humiliation
One of the most widely reported aspects of Mr. al Qahtani's interrogation was the use of sexual, religious, and moral humiliation.

The use of humiliation by U.S. interrogators is best understood by considering illustrative examples, such as the following:

1. Forced nudity, sometimes for prolonged periods and in stress positions;

2. Female interrogators straddling male detainees, invading the personal space of detainees, or otherwise being used in the humiliation of detainees; and

3. Placing leashes on detainees and making them act like dogs.

More specifically, Mr. al Qahtani was subjected to combinations of all of these tactics. The Interrogation Log contains numerous details of Mr. al Qahtani's interrogation. It is important to note, however, that the log is limited in terms of the incidents that it reports, the level of description used (the interrogation log in particular is very sparse and often euphemistic in its descriptions), and the time period covered. Despite these limitations, it is nonetheless clear that the humiliation of Mr. al Qahtani formed a central part of the interrogation plan and that interrogators subjected him to various types of treatment that involved humiliating him, particularly denigrating, either explicitly or implicitly, his religious beliefs. Humiliating treatment designed to degrade Mr. al Qahtani's religious beliefs included:

1. Constructing a shrine to bin Laden and informing Mr. al Qahtani that he could only pray to bin Laden;[3]

2. "Forced grooming,"[4] including forcibly shaving Mr. al Qahtani's beard;[5]

3. Commandeering the call to prayer as a "call to interrogation";[6] and

4. Interrupting Mr. al Qahtani's prayer or attempting to control or deny his right to pray.[7]

The interrogation log explicitly documents several instances when Mohammed al Qahtani is subjected to sexual humiliation techniques:

1. There are at least ten separate instances when the interrogation log reports that interrogators used a technique labeled "invasion of space by a female" or that Mr. al Qahtani is repulsed, angered, or otherwise bothered by a female interrogator invading his personal space. The details of what this involved are generally lacking.[8] "Invasion of Space by a Female" is used to describe a number of tactics, from a female interrogator straddling Mr. al Qahtani and molesting him while other military guards pin his body to the floor against his will, to a female interrogator rubbing his neck and hair, often until Mr. al Qahtani resists with force and is subdued by military guards.

2. There are documented instances of forced nudity.[9]

3. "Dance instruction."

    a. In one incident, a mask was placed on Mr. al Qahtani and he was forced to undergo "dance instruction" with a male interrogator.[10]

    b. In another incident, he was forced to wear a towel "like a burqa" and undergo "dance instruction" with a male interrogator.[11]

4. The interrogators made sexual insults and sexually offensive comments about Mr. al Qahtani and about his female family members, specifically his mother and sisters.[12]

5. Mr. al Qahtani was forced to either wear[13] or to look at and study[14] pornographic pictures. Interrogators required him to memorize details of the pornographic pictures and answer questions as a means to "test" his willingness to cooperate and to end other abusive interrogation practices.

In addition to explicit sexual and religious humiliation, other aspects of Mr. al Qahtani's treatment and detention were also morally humiliating and a denial of his human dignity. This included forcing him to urinate in front of U.S. personnel in either a bottle or in his pants while in restraints[15] and then subsequently denying him the opportunity to clean himself. Military authorities also deprived him of privacy in his living conditions, specifically during showers when both female and male personnel were present.[16] On at least one occasion during an interrogation, he was also stripped and forcibly given an enema while military police restrained him in the presence of multiple U.S. personnel. He was also subjected to the following treatment: "On December 20, 2002 an interrogator tied a leash to the subject of the first Special Interrogation Plan's chains, led him around the room, and forced him to perform a series of dog tricks."[17]

Stress Positions and Temperature Extremes
Mr. al Qahtani reports being restrained with very tight handcuffs in painful positions for extended periods of time, both during the day and night. As noted above, he was left in restraints on numerous occasions until he had no recourse but to urinate on himself. Moreover, he was placed in rooms with very cold temperatures and to this day is sensitive to cold temperatures during attorney-client meetings. At times, Mr. al Qahtani suffered from hypothermia.

Mr. al Qahtani was placed in painful positions for extended times during interrogations that were also accompanied by sleep deprivation, various forms of humiliation, and other abuses.

Threats with Military Dogs
Mr. al Qahtani reports being threatened with military working dogs on several occasions. The interrogation log corroborates Mr. al Qahtani's report, stating that: "issues ar[o]se between MPs and dog handler" on December 7, 2002. In addition to creating a physical danger for the detainees, military dogs were permitted to growl and threaten them as a means of exploiting cultural and individual phobias associated with dogs.

This use of dogs was authorized pursuant to instructions sanctioned by Secretary Rumsfeld—he explicitly authorized the use of dogs as a method of interrogation in the "First Special Interrogation Plan."

The interrogation log and the enclosed information do not describe everything that happened to Mr. al Qahtani. As with many victims of torture, particularly those who have yet to receive any treatment for their physical and psychological injuries, there were many other methods used against him that Mr. al Qahtani cannot yet discuss—and perhaps may choose never to discuss, including some of the methods used to humiliate and degrade his moral and personal integrity.

Additionally, Mr. al Qahtani has no memory of some of the interrogation methods used against him or events that occurred at Guantánamo—evidence that he has not fully recovered from the trauma of his torture and still suffers from its impact. For example, according to new accounts of information leaked by intelligence personnel, Mr. al Qahtani was subjected to a "fake rendition" authorized by Secretary Rumsfeld around April 2003:

> Mr. Kahtani, a Saudi, was given a tranquilizer, put in sensory deprivation garb with blackened goggles, and hustled aboard a plane that was supposedly taking him to the Middle East.
>
> After hours in the air, the plane landed back at the United States naval base at Guantánamo Bay, Cuba, where he was not returned to the regular prison compound but put in an isolation cell in the base's brig. There, he was subjected to harsh interrogation procedures that he was encouraged to believe were being conducted by Egyptian national security operatives.
>
> The account of Mr. Kahtani's treatment given to the *New York Times* recently by military intelligence officials

and interrogators is the latest of several developments that have severely damaged the military's longstanding public version of how the detention and interrogation center at Guantánamo operated.

In order to carry on the charade that he was not at Guantánamo, the military arranged it so Mr. Kahtani was not visited by the Red Cross on a few of its regular visits, creating a window of several months, said a person who dealt with him at Guantánamo.[18]

As a result of the severe physical and psychological torture, Mr. al Qahtani's weight fell from approximately 160 pounds to 100 pounds. During his attorney-client meetings, Mr. al Qahtani also exhibits the signs of an individual suffering from post-traumatic stress syndrome or other trauma-related condition, including memory loss, difficulty concentrating, and anxiety. He is aware that his interrogation has left him physically and mentally injured from the abuse. He will not seek treatment from any health professional at Guantánamo, however, because of their involvement in his interrogation.

He was also hospitalized at least twice when he was close to death during interrogations at Guantánamo. On one occasion described in the interrogation log, he was rushed to a military base hospital when his heart rate fell dangerously low during a period of extreme sleep deprivation, physical stress, and psychological trauma. After being permitted to sleep a full night, medical personnel cleared Mr. al Qahtani for further interrogation the next day. During his transportation from the hospital, Mr. al Qahtani was interrogated in the ambulance.

Mr. al Qahtani strives each day to maintain his mental and physical health while imprisoned at Guantánamo. He must live with the knowledge that the United States government has deprived him, and continues to deprive him, of the most basic of human rights. During our meetings, Mr. al Qahtani has described the fundamental nature of the rights the United States authorities stripped from him:

> A human being needs four things in life that were taken from me at Guantánamo. First, to honor his religion and freedom to practice religion and respect it. Two, honoring his personal dignity by refraining from humiliating a human being through beating or cursing him and bad treatment in general. Three, respect for his honor, which means not dishonoring him through sexual humiliation or abuse. Four, respect for human rights by allowing a human being to sleep and be comfortable where he is, to be in a warm shelter, to have security for his life, to have sufficient food and beverage, to have means to relieve himself and clean his body, to have humane medical treatment, and to know that his family is safe from threats or harm. Again, all of these rights were taken from me.

Mohammed al Qahtani's Torture Log

SECRET ORCON
INTERROGATION LOG
DETAINEE 063

28 November 2002

0400:   SGT R (control) woke detainee up. Detainee drank bottle of water, goes to bathroom and walks. Corpsman checks vitals. Detainee's feet appear more swollen than yesterday. Detainee refused aspirin (offered to help reduce swelling). SGT A (lead) asks detainee about the kicking and spitting incident the night before. Lead explains how detainee has no control.

0415:   Lead begins Al Qaida falling apart theme, goes into pride and ego down. Detainee was repeatedly shown picture of Bin Al Shibh and asked why Bin Al Shibh's life was viewed as being more valuable than his. Detainee told that Bin Al Shibh was viewed as a future leader. Lead wondered out loud why Bin Al Shibh is better than detainee, if Saudis are supposed to be better than Yemenis. Detainee was told he should show Bin Al Shibh respect because he is better than detainee.

0530:   Lead began asking about detainee's family and asking what happened in his household that produced a terrorist. Lead also talked about pictures of 9–11 victims on the wall, focusing on children. Detainee still won't look at lead. Detainee was told that if God keeps track of your sins, he would have millions so he should not be concerned about something as small as looking at a woman.

0615:   Detainee told that he would be going to the bathroom. He said he didn't have to go, but was told that he would go because we wanted him to.

0630:   When control entered booth, detainee stated in English "Excuse me sergeant, I want to pray." Control said "Have you earned prayer? I know you have a lot to ask forgiveness for, but I already told you that you have to earn it." Detainee says "Please, I want to pray here" (pointing to floor next to his chair). Control responds no.

0635:   Detainee placed in swivel chair. As control talked about victims' pictures on wall, MPs rolled detainee to each picture. Particular attention was paid to the children. Control asked "Are these the faces of evil?" Detainee struggled with MPs during his stay in swivel chair. Detainee gets explanation of use of enima—seems embarrassed.

0700:   Control gives Arabic lesson to detainee. Control writes the Arabic words for "liar", "coward", and "failure" on the wall. Control asks detainee "are you a liar? Are you a failure? Are you a coward? Yes you are." Detainee seemed surprised at control's knowledge of Arabic. Control did this in response to detainee's earlier use of english. Detainee said nothing during this session but showed apparent signs of anger toward the theme.

0740:   Control takes break. Medical shows up and checks vitals. Detainee takes walk. Control asks in Arabic "how are you Mohammed?" Detainee responds in arabic "not bad".

0800:   Lead begins session, returning to Al Qaida falling apart. Asks detainee why Bin Al Shibh is better than him.

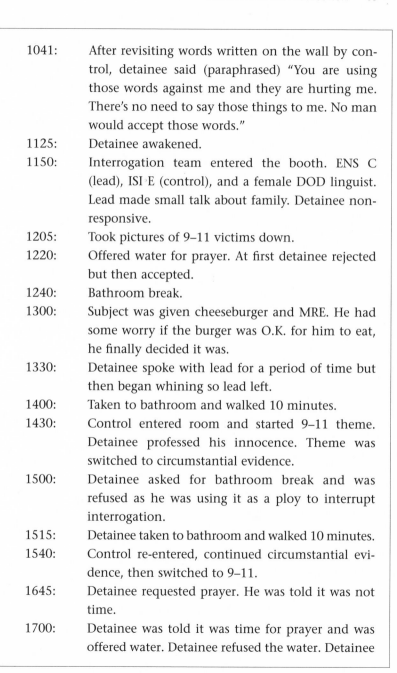

1041:   After revisiting words written on the wall by control, detainee said (paraphrased) "You are using those words against me and they are hurting me. There's no need to say those things to me. No man would accept those words."

1125:   Detainee awakened.

1150:   Interrogation team entered the booth. ENS C (lead), ISI E (control), and a female DOD linguist. Lead made small talk about family. Detainee nonresponsive.

1205:   Took pictures of 9–11 victims down.

1220:   Offered water for prayer. At first detainee rejected but then accepted.

1240:   Bathroom break.

1300:   Subject was given cheeseburger and MRE. He had some worry if the burger was O.K. for him to eat, he finally decided it was.

1330:   Detainee spoke with lead for a period of time but then began whining so lead left.

1400:   Taken to bathroom and walked 10 minutes.

1430:   Control entered room and started 9–11 theme. Detainee professed his innocence. Theme was switched to circumstantial evidence.

1500:   Detainee asked for bathroom break and was refused as he was using it as a ploy to interrupt interrogation.

1515:   Detainee taken to bathroom and walked 10 minutes.

1540:   Control re-entered, continued circumstantial evidence, then switched to 9–11.

1645:   Detainee requested prayer. He was told it was not time.

1700:   Detainee was told it was time for prayer and was offered water. Detainee refused the water. Detainee was then taken to the bathroom and walked 10 minutes. He then said he wanted prayer and would drink. He was told that he could have the water, however the time for prayer had passed.

1750:   Detainee exercised and refused food and water. SGT B began interrogation

1840:   Detainee refused food and water

1900:   Detainee went to the latrine

1945:   SGT M took over interrogation

2000:   Detainee went to the latrine and drank two bottles of water to avoid get an enema

2020:   Detainee exercised by doing knee bends. SGT M implemented SPC P's "Mohammad the Slave" theme. Detainee stated that he is God's slave. Circumstantial evidence theme.

2100:   Detainee exercised and used the latrine

2115:   Interrogation team left detainee to watch 9/11 video

2200:   SGT M taped pictures of the 9/11 victims on detainee's body

2305:   Detainee proclaimed his innocence and said he would pass a polygraph test.

2230:   Detainee went to the latrine

2340:   Detainee exercised

2350:   Medical check

2400:   Detainee drank one bottle of water, used the latrine, and went to bed.

13 December 2002

0001:   Upon entering the booth, lead played the call to prayer with a special alarm clock. Detainee was told, "this is no longer the call to prayer. You're not allowed to pray. This is the call to interrogation. So pay attention." Both lead and control participated in a "pride and ego down" approach. Control told detainee, "UBL has made a whore of Islam. Since you follow UBL, you also rape Islam." Control put a sign on detainee that had the Arabic word for coward written on it. Explained how the words liar, stupid, weak, and failure apply to detainee. Detainee showed very little emotion during the initial portion of the session, except for the occasional smug smile that was met with immediate taunts and ridicule from the interrogators.

0120: Lead ordered detainee to go to bathroom and walk for twenty minutes. Refused Water. Corpsman checked his vital signs and stated he was fine. Both interrogators continued with the "futility" and "pride and ego down" approaches. On occasion when the detainee began to drift off into sleep, lead dripped a couple of drops of water on detainees head to keep him awake. Detainee jerked violently in his chair each time.

0240: After a bathroom and walking break and detainees refusal of water, the interrogators continued the aforementioned approaches. Detainee showed little response during this session. Detainee became increasingly tired and incoherent.

0320: Detainee received walking and bathroom break. Refused water. He then slept for one hour, followed by one hour in his chair listening to white noise.

0530: Control showed detainee the banana rats and stated that they live better than he does. Lead asked detainee, "what do you think is going to happen to you? what would a judge do if he saw all the information that links you to Al-Qaida?" detainee stated, "I'm not associated with Al-Qaida." After that statement, control read all circumstantial evidence collected against detainee. Detainee attempted to hide his emotions, but was clearly frightened when asked if the judge had enough evidence to convict him.

0700:   Detainee walked, refused water, and allowed to begin four hour rest period.

1100:   Detainee awakened and offered coffee—refused.

1115:   Detainee taken to bathroom and walked 10 minutes. Offered water—refused. Interrogators began telling detainee how ungrateful and grumpy he was. In order to escalate the detainee's emotions, a mask was made from an MRE box with a smiley face on it and placed on the detainee's head for a few moments. A latex glove was inflated and labeled the "sissy slap" glove. This glove was touched to the detainee's face periodically after explaining the terminology to him. The mask was placed back on the detainee's head. While wearing the mask, the team began dance instruction with the detainee. The detainee became agitated and began shouting. The mask was removed and detainee was allowed to sit. Detainee shouted and addressed lead as "the oldest Christian here" and wanted to know why lead allowed the detainee to be treated this way.

1300:   Detainee taken to bathroom and walked 10 minutes.

1320:   Detainee offered food and water—refused. Detainee was unresponsive for remainder of session. Afghanistan / Taliban themes run for remainder of session.

1430:   Detainee taken to bathroom and walked 10 minutes.

1500:   Detainee offered water—refused.

1510:   Corpsman changed bandages on ankles, checked vitals—O.K.

1530:   Detainee taken to bathroom and walked 10 minutes.

1600:   Corpsman checks vitals and starts IV. Detainee given three bags of IV.

1745:   Detainee taken to bathroom and walked 10 minutes.

1800:   Detainee was unresponsive.

1833:   Detainee was allowed to sleep.

1925:   The detainee was awakened by interrogation team. He was offered food and water but he refused.

1945:   The interrogation team and detainee watched the video "Operation Enduring Freedom".

2120:   Detainee was sent to the latrine. Offered water but he refused.

2200:   Detainee exercised for good health and circulation. Medical representative took detainee's vital signs and removed the IV housing unit from the detainee's arm. The detainee's pulse rate was low (38) and his blood pressure was high (144/90). Detainee complained of having a boil on his left leg, just below his knee. The medical representative looked at the his leg and phoned the doctor. The doctor instructed the corpsman to recheck the detainee's vitals in one hour.

2300:   Detainee refused water and food. He was taken to the latrine and exercised in order to assist in improving the detainee's vital signs.

2345:   The medical representative rechecked the detainee's vital signs. The detainee's blood pressure had improved but it was still high (138/80) and his pulse rate had improved but it remained low (42). The corpsman called the doctor to provide an update and the doctor said operations could continue since there had been no significant change. It was noted that historically the detainee's pulse sometimes drops into the 40's in the evenings.

Donald Rumsfeld's Memos Authorizing Torture

January 19, 2002

This one-page memorandum from Donald Rumsfeld to the Joint Chiefs of Staff dated January 19, 2002 states that the United States has determined that al Qaeda and the Taliban are to be treated according to the Geneva Conventions "to the extent appropriate and consistent with military necessity." This memo contains the much-contested loophole that arguably permits inhuman treatment if military necessity requires. Rumsfeld and others relied on various legal memos from within the executive branch for this position.

Secretary of Defense

1000 Defense Pentagon

Washington, DC 20301-1000

Jan 19 2002   UNCL

MEMORANDUM FOR CHAIRMAN OF THE JOINT CHIEFS OF STAFF

SUBJECT: Status of Taliban and Al Qaeda

(U) Transmit the following to the Combatant Commanders:
(U) The United States has determined that Al Qaeda and Taliban individuals under the control of the Department of Defense are not entitled to prisoner of war status for purposes of the Geneva Conventions of 1949.
(U) The Combatant Commanders shall, in detaining Al Qaeda and Taliban individuals under the control of the Department of Defense, treat them humanely and, to the extent appropriate and consistent with military necessity, in a manner consistent with the principles of the Geneva Conventions of 1949.
(U) The Combatant Commanders shall transmit this order to subordinate commanders, including Commander, Joint Task Force 160, for implementation.
(U) Keep me appropriately informed of the implementation of this order.

Classified by: SecDef   DECLASSIFIED ON 4 FEB 2002
Reason: 1.5(d)   PER DOD GENERAL COUNCIL MEMO
Declassify on: 01/19/12   Please Notify All Recipients to downgrade
                            this Memorandum to Unclassified

November 27, 2002, and April 16, 2003

These memos concern the approval by Secretary Rumsfeld of various interrogation techniques at Guantánamo. William Haynes, the General Counsel of the Department of Defense, issued the first document, the November 27, 2002, memorandum on counter-resistance techniques, recommending that Secretary Rumsfeld approve the use of techniques for use at Guantánamo such as stress positions, sleep deprivation, isolation for thirty days, deprivation of light and auditory stimuli, twenty-hour interrogations, forced nudity, stripping and hooding, and the use of the fear of dogs to induce stress. Haynes did not, however, approve waterboarding, a technique he had previously found acceptable. Haynes wrote that while even harsher techniques including waterboarding "may be legally available, . . . as a matter of policy, a blanket approval . . . is not warranted at this time." A week later, on December 2, 2002, Secretary Rumsfeld approved all of Haynes' recommendations for use at Guantánamo. Those techniques were subsequently used on detainee Mohammed al Qahtani.

At the bottom of the November 27, 2002, memo is Rumsfeld's infamous scrawled note, in which he states, "However, I stand for 8–10 hours a day. Why is standing limited to 4 hours?"

November 27, 2002

UNCLASSIFIED

GENERAL COUNSEL OF THE DEPARTMENT OF DEFENSE
1000 DEFENSE PENTAGON
WASHINGTON, D. C. 20301-1000

ACTION MEMO

OFFICE OF THE
SECRETARY OF DEFENSE

November 27, 2002 (1:00 PM)
DEPSEC_____

FOR: SECRETARY OF DEFENSE

FROM: William J. Haynes II, General Counsel

SUBJECT: Counter-Resistance Techniques

- The Commander of USSOUTHCOM has forwarded a request by the Commander of Joint Task Force 170 (now JTF GTMO) for approval of counter-resistance techniques to aid in the interrogation of detainees at Guantanamo Bay (Tab A).
- The request contains three categories of counter-resistance techniques, with the first category the least aggressive and the third category the most aggressive (Tab B).
- I have discussed this with the Deputy, Doug Feith and General Myers. I believe that all join in my recommendation that, as a matter of policy, you authorize the Commander of USSOUTHCOM to employ, in his discretion, only Categories I and II and the fourth technique listed in Category III ("Use of mild, non-injurious physical contact such as grabbing, poking in the chest with the finger, and light pushing").
- While all Category III techniques may be legally available, we believe that, as a matter of policy, a blanket approval of Category III techniques is not warranted at this time. Our Armed Forces are trained to a standard of interrogation that reflects a tradition of restraint.

RECOMMENDATION: That SECDEF approve the USSOUTHCOM Commander's use of those counter-resistance techniques listed in Categories I and II and the fourth technique listed in Category III during the interrogation of detainees at Guantanamo Bay.

SECDEF DECISION

Approved ___ Disapproved _____ Other _____

Attachments
As stated

cc: CJCS, USD(P)

However, I stand for 8-10 hours a day. Why is standing limited to 4 hours?

D.R. DEC 0 2 2002

THE SECRETARY OF DEFENSE
1000 DEFENSE PENTAGON
WASHINGTON, DC 20301-1000

MEMORANDUM FOR THE COMMANDER, US SOUTHERN COMMAND

SUBJECT: Counter-Resistance Techniques in the War on Terrorism (S)

(U) I have considered the report of the Working Group that I directed be established on January 15, 2003.

(U) I approve the use of specified counter-resistance techniques, subject to the following:

(U) a. The techniques I authorize are those lettered A-X, set out at Tab A.

(U) b. These techniques must be used with all the safeguards described at Tab B.

(U) c. Use of these techniques is limited to interrogations of unlawful combatants held at Guantanamo Bay, Cuba.

(U) d. Prior to the use of these techniques, the Chairman of the Working Group on Detainee Interrogations in the Global War on Terrorism must brief you and your staff.

(U) I reiterate that US Armed Forces shall continue to treat detainees humanely and, to the extent appropriate and consistent with military necessity, in a manner consistent with the principles of the Geneva Conventions. In addition, if you intend to use techniques B, I, O, or X, you must specifically determine that military necessity requires its use and notify me in advance.

(U) If, in your view, you require additional interrogation techniques for a particular detainee, you should provide me, via the Chairman of the Joint Chiefs of Staff, a written request describing the proposed technique, recommended safeguards, and the rationale for applying it with an identified detainee.

(U) Nothing in this memorandum in any way restricts your existing authority to maintain good order and discipline among detainees.

Attachments:
As stated

	Classified By: Secretary of Defense
NOT RELEASABLE TO	Reason: 1.5(a)
FOREIGN NATIONALS	Declassify On: 2 April 2013

INTERROGATION TECHNIQUES

(U) The use of techniques A - X is subject to the general safeguards as provided below as well as specific implementation guidelines to be provided by the appropriate authority. Specific implementation guidance with respect to techniques A - Q is provided in Army Field Manual 34-52. Further implementation guidance with respect to techniques R - X will need to be developed by the appropriate authority.

(U) Of the techniques set forth below, the policy aspects of certain techniques should be considered to the extent those policy aspects reflect the views of other major U.S. partner nations. Where applicable, the description of the technique is annotated to include a summary of the policy issues that should be considered before application of the technique.

A. (U) Direct: Asking straightforward questions.

B. (U) Incentive/Removal of Incentive: Providing a reward or removing a privilege, above and beyond those that are required by the Geneva Convention, from detainees. [Caution: Other nations that believe that detainees are entitled to POW protections may consider that provision and retention of religious items (e.g., the Koran) are protected under international law (see, Geneva III, Article 34). Although the provisions of the Geneva Convention are not applicable to the interrogation of unlawful combatants, consideration should be given to these views prior to application of the technique.]

C. (U) Emotional Love: Playing on the love a detainee has for an individual or group.

D. (U) Emotional Hate: Playing on the hatred a detainee has for an individual or group.

E. (U) Fear Up Harsh: Significantly increasing the fear level in a detainee.

F. (U) Fear Up Mild: Moderately increasing the fear level in a detainee.

G. (U) Reduced Fear: Reducing the fear level in a detainee.

H. (U) Pride and Ego Up: Boosting the ego of a detainee.

Classified By: Secretary of Defense
Reason: 1.5(a)
Declassify On: 2 April 2013

I. (U) Pride and Ego Down: Attacking or insulting the ego of a detainee, not beyond the limits that would apply to a POW. [Caution: Article 17 of Geneva III provides, "Prisoners of war who refuse to answer may not be threatened, insulted, or exposed to any unpleasant or disadvantageous treatment of any kind." Other nations that believe that detainees are entitled to POW protections may consider this technique inconsistent with the provisions of Geneva. Although the provisions of Geneva are not applicable to the interrogation of unlawful combatants, consideration should be given to these views prior to application of the technique.]

J. (U) Futility: Invoking the feeling of futility of a detainee.

K. (U) We Know All: Convincing the detainee that the interrogator knows the answer to questions he asks the detainee.

L. (U) Establish Your Identity: Convincing the detainee that the interrogator has mistaken the detainee for someone else.

M. (U) Repetition Approach: Continuously repeating the same question to the detainee within interrogation periods of normal duration.

N. (U) File and Dossier: Convincing detainee that the interrogator has a damning and inaccurate file, which must be fixed.

O. (U) Mutt and Jeff: A team consisting of a friendly and harsh interrogator. The harsh interrogator might employ the Pride and Ego Down technique. [Caution: Other nations that believe that POW protections apply to detainees may view this technique as inconsistent with Geneva III, Article 13 which provides that POWs must be protected against acts of intimidation. Although the provisions of Geneva are not applicable to the interrogation of unlawful combatants, consideration should be given to these views prior to application of the technique.]

P. (U) Rapid Fire: Questioning in rapid succession without allowing detainee to answer.

Q. (U) Silence: Staring at the detainee to encourage discomfort.

R. (U) Change of Scenery Up: Removing the detainee from the standard interrogation setting (generally to a location more pleasant, but no worse).

S. (U) Change of Scenery Down: Removing the detainee from the standard interrogation setting and placing him in a setting that may be less comfortable; would not constitute a substantial change in environmental quality.

T. (U) Dietary Manipulation: Changing the diet of a detainee; no intended deprivation of food or water; no adverse medical or cultural effect and without intent to deprive subject of food or water, e.g., hot rations to MREs.

U. (U) Environmental Manipulation: Altering the environment to create moderate discomfort (e.g., adjusting temperature or introducing an unpleasant smell). Conditions would not be such that they would injure the detainee. Detainee would be accompanied by interrogator at all times. [Caution: Based on court cases in other countries, some nations may view application of this technique in certain circumstances to be inhumane. Consideration of these views should be given prior to use of this technique.]

V. (U) Sleep Adjustment: Adjusting the sleeping times of the detainee (e.g., reversing sleep cycles from night to day.) This technique is NOT sleep deprivation.

W. (U) False Flag: Convincing the detainee that individuals from a country other than the United States are interrogating him.

X. (U) Isolation: Isolating the detainee from other detainees while still complying with basic standards of treatment. [Caution: The use of isolation as an interrogation technique requires detailed implementation instructions, including specific guidelines regarding the length of isolation, medical and psychological review, and approval for extensions of the length of isolation by the appropriate level in the chain of command. This technique is not known to have been generally used for interrogation purposes for longer than 30 days. Those nations that believe detainees are subject to POW protections may view use of this technique as inconsistent with the requirements of Geneva III, Article 13 which provides that POWs must be protected against acts of intimidation; Article 14 which provides that POWs are entitled to respect for their person; Article 34 which prohibits coercion and Article 126 which ensures access and basic standards of treatment. Although the provisions of Geneva are not applicable to the interrogation of unlawful combatants, consideration should be given to these views prior to application of the technique.]

GENERAL SAFEGUARDS

(U) Application of these interrogation techniques is subject to the following general safeguards: (i) limited to use only at strategic interrogation facilities; (ii) there is a good basis to believe that the detainee possesses critical intelligence; (iii) the detainee is medically and operationally evaluated as suitable (considering all techniques to be used in combination); (iv) interrogators are specifically trained for the technique(s); (v) a specific interrogation plan (including reasonable safeguards, limits on duration, intervals between applications, termination criteria and the presence or availability of qualified medical personnel) has been developed; (vi) there is appropriate supervision; and, (vii) there is appropriate specified senior approval for use with any specific detainee (after considering the foregoing and receiving legal advice).

(U) The purpose of all interviews and interrogations is to get the most information from a detainee with the least intrusive method, always applied in a humane and lawful manner with sufficient oversight by trained investigators or interrogators. Operating instructions must be developed based on command policies to insure uniform, careful, and safe application of any interrogations of detainees.

(U) Interrogations must always be planned, deliberate actions that take into account numerous, often interlocking factors such as a detainee's current and past performance in both detention and interrogation, a detainee's emotional and physical strengths and weaknesses, an assessment of possible approaches that may work on a certain detainee in an effort to gain the trust of the detainee, strengths and weaknesses of interrogators, and augmentation by other personnel for a certain detainee based on other factors.

(U) Interrogation approaches are designed to manipulate the detainee's emotions and weaknesses to gain his willing cooperation. Interrogation operations are never conducted in a vacuum: they are conducted in close cooperation with the units detaining the individuals. The policies established by the detaining units that pertain to searching, silencing, and segregating also play a role in the interrogation of a detainee. Detainee interrogation involves developing a plan tailored to an individual and approved by senior interrogators. Strict adherence to policies/standard operating procedures governing the administration of interrogation techniques and oversight is essential.

Classified By: Secretary of Defense
Reason: 1.5(a)
Declassify On: 2 April 2013

(U) It is important that interrogators be provided reasonable latitude to vary techniques depending on the detainee's culture, strengths, weaknesses, environment, extent of training in resistance techniques as well as the urgency of obtaining information that the detainee is known to have.

(U) While techniques are considered individually within this analysis, it must be understood that in practice, techniques are usually used in combination; the cumulative effect of all techniques to be employed must be considered before any decisions are made regarding approval for particular situations. The title of a particular technique is not always fully descriptive of a particular technique. With respect to the employment of any techniques involving physical contact, stress or that could produce physical pain or harm, a detailed explanation of that technique must be provided to the decision authority prior to any decision.

Schlesinger Report Chart of Techniques Authorized by Donald Rumsfeld

The following document is a chart taken from the Schlesinger Report that details the evolution of interrogation techniques at Guantánamo, listing what techniques were approved by Donald Rumsfeld and when he approved them. The acronym "FM 34-53" in the headings refers to the U.S. Army Field Manual on Interrogation and shows which interrogation techniques were permitted by the field manual. The techniques approved by Donald Rumsfeld go much further than the Field Manual, as the chart details.

Evolution of Interrogation Techniques - GTMO

Interrogation Techniques	FM 34-52 (1992) Jan 02–01 Dec 02	Secretary of Defense Approved Tiered System 02 Dec 02–15 Jan 03	FM 34-52 (1992) with some Cat I 16 Jan 03–15 Apr 03	Secretary of Defense Memo 16 Apr 03 – Present
Direct questioning	X	X	X	X
Incentive/removal of incentive	X	X	X	X
Emotional love	X	X	X	X
Emotional hate	X	X	X	X
Fear up harsh	X	X	X	X
Fear up mild	X	X	X	X
Reduced fear	X	X	X	X
Pride and ego up	X	X	X	X
Pride and ego down	X	X	X	X
Futility	X	X	X	X
We know all	X	X	X	X
Establish your identity	X	X	X	X
Repetition approach	X	X	X	X
File and dossier	X	X	X	X
Mutt and Jeff				X*
Rapid Fire	X	X	X	X
Silence	X	X	X	X
Change of Scene	X	X	X	X
Yelling		X (Cat I)	X	
Deception		X (Cat I)		
Multiple interrogators		X (Cat I)		

(continued)

Evolution of Interrogation Techniques - GTMO (Continued)

Interrogation Techniques	FM 34-52 (1992) Jan 02–01 Dec 02	Secretary of Defense Approved Tiered System 02 Dec 02–15 Jan 03	FM 34-52 (1992) with some Cat I 16 Jan 03–15 Apr 03	Secretary of Defense Memo 16 Apr 03 – Present
Interrogator identity		X (Cat I)	X	
Stress positions, like standing		X (Cat II)		
False documents/reports		X (Cat II)		
Isolation for up to 30 days		X (Cat II)		X*
Deprivation of light/auditory stimuli		X (Cat II)		
Hooding (transportation & questioning)		X (Cat II)		
20-interrogations		X (Cat II)		
Removal of ALL comfort items, including religious items				
MRE-only diet		X (Cat II)		X*
Removal of clothing		X (Cat II)		
Forced grooming		X (Cat II)		
Exploiting individual phobias, e.g. dogs		X (Cat II)		
Mild, non-injurious physical contact, e.g. grabbing, poking or light pushing		X (Cat III)		
Environmental manipulation				X
Sleep adjustment				X
False flag				X

*Techniques require SOUTHCOM approval and SECDEF notification.
Source: Naval IG Investigation Appendix E.

FROM GUANTÁNAMO TO ABU GHRAIB: THE EXPORT OF ILLEGAL INTERROGATION TECHNIQUES FROM WASHINGTON AND GUANTÁNAMO TO IRAQ

Following the invasion of Iraq by U.S.-led troops, the question for the political and military authorities in Washington and Baghdad was how to deal with prisoners of war and so-called "illegal combatants." As at Guantánamo Bay, the focus of official interest was to obtain actionable intelligence from the prisoners. A February 2004 report by the International Committee of the Red Cross stated that ill-treatment of prisoners by military personnel in Iraq occurred systematically.[19] And, according to official government-sponsored reports, the entire military chain of command was involved in the implementation of interrogation methods that were similar to those used at Guantánamo.

In August 2003, Rumsfeld himself directed his top assistant on intelligence issues, Stephen Cambone, to send Major General Miller, the commander with authority over interrogations at Guantánamo Bay, to Iraq in order to "review current Iraqi Theater ability to rapidly exploit internees for actionable intelligence."[20] Major General Miller was authorized to conform interrogation methods in Iraq to those at Guantánamo. Abu Ghraib commander and former Brigadier General Janis Karpinski has said that when she met with Miller during his initial visit to Abu Ghraib in September 2003, Miller told her he was going to "Gitmo-ize" the prison. In consequence, in Iraqi prison camps, detention and intelligence functions were largely integrated, and existing interrogation methods were subject to reappraisal and reevaluation. After arriving in Iraq in September, Miller gave his April 16, 2003, tactical guidelines for Guantánamo to Combined Joint Task Force 7 (CJTF-7), which was under the command of Lieutenant General Ricardo Sanchez. He recommended this as a possible model for an Iraq-wide policy. These guidelines were subsequently approved by the Abu Ghraib commander and put into practice. This meant, however, that special illegal techniques that were developed at Guantánamo—including the use of dogs and stripping detainees—outside the legal framework of the Geneva Conventions protections were exported wholesale to Iraq, without being reviewed, updated, or modified to conform to a situation in which even the Bush administration admitted the Geneva Conventions were to be "fully applied." In short, Secretary of Defense Rumsfeld illegally agreed to a program for the use of violence in interrogating predominantly non-al Qaeda prisoners in Iraq that was originally designed as a "special" program for al Qaeda suspects. Rumsfeld did not inform Congress of this measure.

Miller's transfer to Abu Ghraib to develop an effective interrogation policy played a significant part in the implementation of interrogation practices that violated human rights. In autumn of 2003, Ricardo Sanchez, commander of Army Corps V and CJTF-7, authorized the use of cruel and inhuman interrogation methods against prisoners that went far beyond army regulations and violated the Geneva Conventions—including isolation for long periods of time, exposure to extreme temperatures, reversal of sleep patterns, sensory deprivation, stress positions, shackling, forced stripping, and manipulation of nutrition. When the military central command declared the September directive to be too aggressive and, in part, incompatible with existing principles, Sanchez quickly revoked it and issued a new version that was only slightly less harsh. Sanchez trusted the advice of his staff judge advocate, Marc Warren, that he had the authority to issue such a directive and to make decisions on whether and how prisoners were to be placed under the protection of the Geneva Conventions.

Sanchez knew of the abuses occurring in detention facilities under his command in late summer 2003 at the latest, through the Ryder Report and the Report of the International Committee of the Red Cross. In 2003, Sanchez visited Abu Ghraib prison several times, and was supposedly even present at some interrogations. However, he failed to end the abuse and other war crimes. In the official military investigation, Sanchez was accused of having done nothing to improve the situation at Abu Ghraib.

As noted in the indictments, Sanchez largely delegated responsibility to his deputy, Major General Wojdakowski. Wojdakowski not only directly authorized illegal interrogation methods; in the military chain of command, he held a position as superior that made him directly responsible for abuses committed by military personnel, and that would have allowed him to prevent the abuses. According to a *Washington Post* report on May 26, 2004, the interrogation plans providing for use of dogs, shackling, stripping of prisoners, and similar aggressive measures were often authorized by Sanchez's deputy Wojdakowski or Colonel Thomas Pappas. According to Karpinski's testimony, when the Red Cross complained in a report about specific cases of abuse and human rights violations in Abu Ghraib, Wojdakowski was among the people who discussed the report at length in a meeting.

As commander of the 205th Military Intelligence Brigade and commander of Abu Ghraib from November 2003 to February 2004, Colonel Pappas had effective command authority over those who committed the abuse. The Taguba Report concluded that Pappas was responsible for the acts of all his subordinates— at least because he was aware that war crimes were taking place in Abu Ghraib. He visited the prison regularly and twice refused Red

Cross teams access to specific prisoners. On November 4, 2003, Iraqi prisoner al-Jamadi died while handcuffed, face down, in Abu Ghraib while being interrogated by a CIA officer and marines. Captain Donald J. Reese, Commander of the 372nd Military Police Company, later testified that Pappas was with a group of intelligence officers who stood around the bloody body of a prisoner and discussed what to do.

Before April 2004, the gigantic Abu Ghraib prison, twenty miles west of Baghdad, was known as a symbol of Saddam Hussein's inhuman and dictatorial regime. This was the place where Iraqi prisoners routinely suffered torture and cruel treatment. It was also, in 2003, one of the symbols used by the Bush administration to justify the need to bring Hussein's regime down.

How ironic then, that—since April 2004 when the photographs of torture by *Americans* against Iraqis at Abu Ghraib were reported worldwide—Abu Ghraib now represents the complete failure of the United States to apply the very standards of humanity it claims it fought to ensure.

But the torture at Abu Ghraib was no accident, nor the actions of a few "bad guys." Torture at Abu Ghraib followed a strategy thought through well in advance and ordered from the very top of the military and civilian chain of command. It was a decision—based on orders—to "break down" Iraqi detainees, by all means—finding ways to torture detainees without cutting off their fingers, and simultaneously redefining torture so narrowly as to make the term all but meaningless.

The acts of torture—it was no less than torture—were first reported through shocking and graphic pictures showing sadistic treatment: piles of naked bodies, men forced to simulate sexual acts, men covered with excrement, men on the ground with their hands tied in the back while they were being beaten by guards, detainees about to be subjected to electric shocks, military dogs threatening to attack detainees, and so on. The report on this torture written in January 2004 by General Taguba, and leaked in

April 2004, found numerous cases of "sadistic, blatant and wanton criminal abuses" at Abu Ghraib.[21] Abuses included:

> Pouring the phosphoric liquid on detainees; pouring cold water on naked detainees; beating detainees with a broom handle and a chair; threatening male detainees with rape; allowing a military police guard to stitch the wound of a detainee who was injured after being slammed against the wall in his cell; sodomizing a detainee with a chemical light and perhaps a broom stick, and using military working dogs to frighten and intimidate detainees with threats of attack.

Yet these atrocities were only the tip of the iceberg. The worst pictures were not initially released publicly, as they depicted acts of rape and homicide. Videotapes of Americans sodomizing Iraqi boys were suppressed by the Bush administration in 2004.[22] Likewise, the Bush administration kept from the public evidence that abuses took place not only in Abu Ghraib, but in other U.S.-controlled detention centers in Iraq, in Afghanistan, at Guantánamo Bay, and in secret sites worldwide. In November 2003, Rumsfeld ordered military officials in Iraq to detain high-level suspects without registering them on the prison's rolls, in order to hide them from the monitoring of the Red Cross, in violation of their international obligations under the Geneva Conventions. Prisoners were held in at least a dozen facilities operating secretly; the Pentagon later admitted these facts publicly.[23] The Schlesinger Report confirmed in August 2004 that abuses were "widespread," "serious both in number and in effect," and that there is both "institutional and personal responsibility at higher levels."[24]

Numerous abuses and deaths of detainees at the U.S.-controlled Bagram Air Base in Afghanistan were also later reported, confirming the pattern of abuse. In December 2002, two inmates were tortured to death in their cells. They had been "[h]ung by their arms from the ceiling and beaten so severely that, according to a report by Army investigators later leaked to the *Baltimore Sun*, their legs would have needed to be amputated had they lived."[25]

A man who was detained at Bagram Air Base in 2002–2003 stated that "an American soldier took me blindfolded. My hands were tightly cuffed, with my ears plugged so I could not hear properly, and my mouth covered so I could only make a muffled scream. Two soldiers, one on each side, forced me to bend down, and a third pressed my face down over a table. A fourth soldier then pulled down my trousers. They rammed a stick up my rectum."[26]

After looking into what was occurring at Abu Ghraib and elsewhere, one better understands why, the year before, the Department of Justice and the White House, pressed by Vice President Dick Cheney, fought so hard in various confidential memos to argue that there was a critical (and entirely novel) distinction between "torture" and "cruel, inhuman, and degrading" methods of questioning, the latter category being considered admissible by the Bush administration. Rather than representing the aberrant behavior of individual soldiers including Lynndie England and Charles Graner, notable for having photographed their own atrocities, the abuse captured in the Abu Ghraib footage represents the Bush administration's intended treatment of detainees in the context of the "war on terror," authorized at the highest possible levels.

Stories of Iraqi Plaintiffs

The following document contains descriptions of the abuse and torture of three Iraqis detained at prisons in Iraq, including Abu Ghraib, and tortured by U.S. military personnel. The document was prepared in conjunction with the three men in preparation for filing of court papers and reflects statements the three made to their attorneys about their treatment. These three men, like hundreds of others, still have not seen justice.

Ahmed Shehab Ahmed, is an Iraqi citizen from Baghdad born on January 1, 1968. He is a trader by profession and described himself as a politically independent Muslim. He was arrested in his home by personnel of the U.S. Armed Forces. At this time his 80-year-old handicapped father was shot and killed and valuables were stolen from the house. He was at first held at Baghdad International Airport and then brought to Rehidwaniya, an old property of Saddam Hussein. There he was beaten and stripped. He was deprived of sleep and food, and had to survive three days without sanitary facilities. During his detention he was threatened with rape, beaten until unconscious, and forbidden to pray. He was doused with cold water. Soldiers injected his genitalia with unidentified substances. An American officer held a loudspeaker to his ears and shouted at him, so that the plaintiff lost his hearing. During an interrogation with a female translator he was naked and only his head was hooded. In the course of this interrogation the interrogator and interpreter attempted sexual acts with him. As a consequence of this sexual abuse he has become impotent. He was threatened with the rape of his family and children. Upon his release, he was told that they were sorry, that they had false information about him and his father.

Hamid Ahmed Khalaf Harej Al-Zeidi, an Iraqi Muslim born on Jul. 1st, 1966, was detained by American forces from Oct. 9th,

2003, until May 28th, 2004, in Abu Ghraib (Camp A, the solitary cell No. 12, Tent 1, Camp B, the solitary cell No. 56, Room No. 10, and then room No. 2, Tent No. 1-10, No. 151417). He was stripped naked and kept in a solitary room for 12 days without food, very little water, was denied sleep, prayer and access to the bathroom. He was repeatedly stripped naked, forced to walk in front of other prisoners and then photographed. He was punched, beaten up with cables, sticks and rods. He was forced to stand or sit in painful positions for lengthy periods of time. Americans threatened to rape and kill him and his family. He had soldiers touching his genitalia. He witnessed many acts of torture and rapes of several co-detainees.

Ziyad Abdul Majeed Al-Jenabi, an Iraqi Muslim born on Jun. 6th, 1950, was detained by American forces from Dec 21th, 2003, until Jun. 15th, 2004, in Falluja, Mujahiddi Khaleq (No. 7422) and Abu Ghraib (Camp 2-1, Tent 4-16, No. 156325). For four days in the winter, he was put in a small room with no ceiling, was denied food, water and clothing. He was forced to stand or sit in painful positions for lengthy periods of time, including chained on a "torture chair" for 10 hours. Many times, because of such mistreatment, he lost consciousness and was once taken to the hospital. He was also threatened by dogs. Americans threatened to rape and kill him and his family. The plaintiff was forced by the soldiers to witness the torture of his son to make him confess, while he also witnessed the mistreatment of many other co-detainees.

The Taguba Report

This document is composed of key excerpts from a report drafted by Major General Antonio M. Taguba, commonly called the Taguba Report, that investigated the abuse and torture of prisoners at the Abu Ghraib prison in Baghdad by members of the 800th Military Police Brigade between October and December 2003. The report was ordered by Lt. Gen. Ricardo Sanchez, commander of Joint Task Force-7, the senior U.S. military official in Iraq, following persistent allegations of human rights abuses at the prison. The report found that torture and abuse were widespread, and recommended increased training for interrogators and adherence to the Geneva Conventions. It was issued October 19, 2004.

[B]etween October and December 2003, at the Abu Ghraib Confinement Facility (BCCF), numerous incidents of sadistic, blatant, and wanton criminal abuses were inflicted on several detainees. This systemic and illegal abuse of detainees was intentionally perpetrated by several members of the military police guard force (372nd Military Police Company, 320th Military Police Battalion, 800th MP Brigade), in Tier (section) 1-A of the Abu Ghraib Prison (BCCF).

In addition, several detainees also described the following acts of abuse, which under the circumstances, I find credible based on the clarity of their statements and supporting evidence provided by other witnesses

    a. Breaking chemical lights and pouring the phosphoric liquid on detainees;

    b. Threatening detainees with a charged 9mm pistol;

    c. Pouring cold water on naked detainees;

    d. Beating detainees with a broom handle and a chair;

    e. Threatening male detainees with rape;

    f. Allowing a military police guard to stitch the wound of a detainee who was injured after being slammed against the wall in his cell;

g. Sodomizing a detainee with a chemical light and perhaps a broom stick;

h. Using military working dogs to frighten and intimidate detainees with threats of attack, and in one instance actually biting a detainee.

[T]he intentional abuse of detainees by military police personnel included the following acts:

a. Punching, slapping, and kicking detainees; jumping on their naked feet;

b. Videotaping and photographing naked male and female detainees;

c. Forcibly arranging detainees in various sexually explicit positions for photographing;

d. Forcing detainees to remove their clothing and keeping them naked for several days at a time;

e. Forcing naked male detainees to wear women's underwear;

f. Forcing groups of male detainees to masturbate themselves while being photographed and videotaped;

g. Arranging naked male detainees in a pile and then jumping on them;

h. Positioning a naked detainee on a MRE Box, with a sandbag on his head, and attaching wires to his fingers, toes, and penis to simulate electric torture;

i. Writing "I am a Rapest" [sic] on the leg of a detainee alleged to have forcibly raped a 15-year-old fellow detainee, and then photographing him naked;

j. Placing a dog chain or strap around a naked detainee's neck and having a female Soldier pose for a picture;

k. A male MP guard having sex with a female detainee;

l. Using military working dogs (without muzzles) to intimidate and frighten detainees, and in at least one case biting and severely injuring a detainee;

m. Taking photographs of dead Iraqi detainees.

These findings are amply supported by written confessions provided by several of the suspects, written statements provided by detainees, and witness statements.

The various detention facilities operated by the 800th MP Brigade have routinely held persons brought to them by Other Government Agencies (OGAs) without accounting for them, knowing their identities, or even the reason for their detention. The Joint Interrogation and Debriefing Center (JIDC) at Abu Ghraib called these detainees "ghost detainees." On at least one occasion, the 320th MP Battalion at Abu Ghraib held a handful of "ghost detainees" for OGAs that they moved around within the facility to hide them from a visiting International Committee of the Red Cross (ICRC) survey team. This maneuver was deceptive, contrary to Army Doctrine, and in violation of international law.

There is abundant evidence in the statements of numerous witnesses that soldiers throughout the 800th MP Brigade were not proficient in their basic MOS [Military Occupational Specialty] skills, particularly regarding internment/resettlement operations. Moreover, there is no evidence that the command, although aware of these deficiencies, attempted to correct them in any systemic manner other than ad hoc training by individuals with civilian corrections experience.

With respect to the 800th MP Brigade mission at Abu Ghraib (BCCF),[27] I find that there was clear friction and lack of effective communication between the Commander, 205th MI Brigade, who controlled FOB Abu Ghraib (BCCF) after 19 November 2003, and the Commander, 800th MP Brigade, who controlled detainee operations inside the FOB. There was no clear delineation of responsibility between commands, little coordination at the command level, and no integration of the two functions. Coordination occurred at the lowest possible levels with little oversight by commanders.

BG Karpinski alleged that she received no help from the Civil Affairs Command, specifically, no assistance from either BG John

Kern or COL Tim Regan. She blames much of the abuse that occurred in Abu Ghraib (BCCF) on MI personnel and stated that MI personnel had given the MPs "ideas" that led to detainee abuse. In addition, she blamed the 372nd Company Platoon Sergeant, SFC Snider, the Company Commander, CPT Reese, and the First Sergeant, MSG Lipinski, for the abuse. She argued that problems in Abu Ghraib were the fault of COL Pappas and LTC Jordan because COL Pappas was in charge of FOB Abu Ghraib.

RECOMMENDATIONS AS TO PART THREE
OF THE INVESTIGATION:
That **COL Thomas M. Pappas, Commander, 205th MI Brigade**, be given a General Officer Memorandum of Reprimand and Investigated UP Procedure 15, AR 381-10, US Army Intelligence Activities for the following acts which have been previously referred to in the aforementioned findings:

- Failing to ensure that Soldiers under his direct command were properly trained in and followed the IROE.
- Failing to ensure that Soldiers under his direct command knew, understood, and followed the protections afforded to detainees in the Geneva Convention Relative to the Treatment of Prisoners of War.
- Failing to properly supervise his soldiers working and "visiting" Tier 1 of the Hard-Site at Abu Ghraib (BCCF).

Democracy Now! Interview with Former U.S. Army Interrogator Tony Lagouranis

This document is an excerpt from the transcript of an interview that Amy Goodman conducted on Democracy Now! *in November, 2005, with former U.S. army interrogator Tony Lagouranis, who went to Iraq in January 2004. Lagouranis speaks about his involvement with abusing detainees in Iraq and torture carried out by the Navy SEALs. In this interview, he apologizes to the Iraqi people and urges U.S. soldiers to follow their conscience. Lagouranis returned from Iraq in January 2005. This excerpt focuses on specific interrogation techniques as well as who Lagouranis thinks ultimately is to blame for the torture of Iraqi prisoners.*

AMY GOODMAN: Tony, can you talk about the use of dogs?

TONY LAGOURANIS: We were using dogs in the Mosul detention facility which was at the Mosul airport. We would put the prisoner in a shipping container. We would keep him up all night with music and strobe lights, stress positions, and then we would bring in dogs. The prisoner was blindfolded, so he didn't really understand what was going on, but we had the dog controlled. He was being held by a military police dog handler on a leash, and the dog was muzzled, so he couldn't hurt the prisoner. That was the only time I ever saw dogs used in Iraq.

AMY GOODMAN: Did the prisoner know that there was a muzzle on the dog?

TONY LAGOURANIS: No, because he was blindfolded. So, the dog would be barking and jumping on the prisoner, and the prisoner wouldn't really understand what was going on.

AMY GOODMAN: What did you think of this practice that you were engaging in?

TONY LAGOURANIS: Well, I knew that we were really walking the line, and I was going through the interrogation rules of engagement that was given to me by the unit that we were working with up there, trying to figure out what was legal and what wasn't legal. According to this interrogation rules of engagement, that was legal. So, when they ordered me to do it, I had to do it. You know, as far as whether, you know, I thought it was a good interrogation practice, I didn't think so at all, actually. We never produced any intelligence.

AMY GOODMAN: At this point when you got there, the photos were out. If not out to the public, they came out in April of 2004, certainly being circulated among soldiers. Had you seen pictures?

TONY LAGOURANIS: I only saw the pictures when they came out on the news. In fact, I was up there using the dogs like at the very time that the scandal broke. But I don't think those pictures were being circulated among soldiers. I mean, I certainly never saw them before they came out on *60 Minutes*.

AMY GOODMAN: So, when you saw them, and you yourself were engaging in this practice, what were your thoughts?

TONY LAGOURANIS: I think my initial reaction was that these were bad apples, like the White House line, but you know, it's funny, like I didn't really tie it to what we were doing up there. We were using some pretty harsh methods on the prisoners. I had seen other units that were using— like, really severe methods, but I didn't tie it to the scandal. It just seemed like—I don't know why. I don't know.

. . .

AMY GOODMAN: Did you use hypothermia as a means of interrogating?

TONY LAGOURANIS: We did. Yeah, we used hypothermia a lot. It was very cold up in Mosul at that time, so we—it was also raining a lot, so we would keep the prisoner outside, and they would have a polyester jumpsuit on and they would be wet and cold, and freezing. But we weren't inducing hypothermia with ice water like the SEALS were. But, you know, maybe the SEALS were doing it better than we were, because they were actually even controlling it with the thermometer, but we weren't doing that.

AMY GOODMAN: At what point did you start to ask questions? When you say about the pictures that you didn't associate what you did with the scandal of the photographs that had come out, but when did you start to say—is this right?

TONY LAGOURANIS: Well, I always was, and it's funny, Amy, because I was sort of pushing to back away from the harsh tactics, but at the same time I was—in a way, I sort of wanted to push, because we were frustrated by, you know, not getting intel. I don't know why. So, I was on both sides of the fence. I don't know.

AMY GOODMAN: Were you having discussions with other interrogators?

TONY LAGOURANIS: Sure. We all talked about it. I discussed this with my team leader all the time. The people I was working with all the time. You know part of the problem back then too, is that I was still under the impression that we were getting prisoners who had intel—who had intel to give us, and you know, I still thought that these were bad guys.

I was believing the intelligence reports that came in with the prisoner. I believed the detainee units, but later it became clear to me that they weren't—they were picking up just farmers, you know, like these guys were totally innocent and that's why we weren't getting intel. And it just made what we were doing, like, seem even more cruel.

AMY GOODMAN: You said that you engaged in abuse, specifically what did you feel was your most egregious abuses that you engaged in?

TONY LAGOURANIS: Well, as I said, in Mosul, I was using dogs and hypothermia, I was using sleep deprivation, isolation, dietary manipulation, you know, that's all abuse, according to the army field manual, the army doctrine and certainly according to the Geneva Conventions.

AMY GOODMAN: Did you ever call for a stop to this, or ask to speak to a higher up?

TONY LAGOURANIS: I did all the time. You know, at that point, I was like so pissed at the military for what they were doing, you know. And you know, I was yelling at the chief warrant officer marine who was in charge of the defense facility. I was making an issue about it to the major of the Marines, and the lieutenant colonel who was the JAG guy who was in charge of release, who organize keeping the prisoners. I mean, but they just wouldn't listen. You know? They wanted numbers. They wanted numbers of terrorists, apprehended at FOB CALSU, so they could brief that to the general.

. . .

AMY GOODMAN: What when you look back now, do you wish you had done?

TONY LAGOURANIS: Well, you know, we were trained to do interrogations according to the Geneva Conventions with enemy prisoners of war. And we trained using role players, using a conventional army prisoner, and also a terrorist organization, and we treated both of them as though they were enemy prisoners of war. We weren't allowed to cross any lines. So, I don't know why I allowed the army to order me to go against my training, and against my better judgment and against my own moral judgment. But I did. I should have just said no.

AMY GOODMAN: Would you say when you see the court-martial of a few low-level soldiers, would you say that will start to stop the abuse, or how high up do you feel it goes?

TONY LAGOURANIS: Well, it obviously goes right up to the Pentagon, because they were issuing the interrogation rules of engagement, and the interrogation rules of engagement are not in accordance with the army field manual and not in accordance with the Geneva Conventions. So, it's all the way up. You know, obviously, Lynndie England and Grainer [sic], these guys—you know, they needed to be punished, but it's not just them. It's—it should have gone all the way up the chain.

COMMAND RESPONSIBILITY

The war crimes trials held after World War II established the modern-day responsibility of superiors and high-level officials for crimes committed by their subordinates on their watch, regardless of whether the officers were personally involved in abuse. Since then, it has become well established under international and American law that individual criminal responsibility is not limited to persons who have directly committed a crime.

As leading constitutional scholar Jules Lobel pointed out in an affidavit submitted as part of the German case against Donald Rumsfeld, command responsibility has two distinct components:

- the liability of a superior for giving unlawful orders to his subordinates or for soliciting, inducing, or otherwise aiding and abetting a crime. In fact, the individual who orders an international crime "is not a mere accomplice but rather a perpetrator by means, using a subordinate to commit the crime."[28]

- the imputed criminal responsibility for a crime committed by a subordinate over whom the superior had effective control, arising from a superior's failure to prevent or punish a crime he knew was about to or had been committed. This can include the responsibility of a commander for failing to ensure that his MPs are appropriately trained for interrogations.

But, despite the very clear state of the law on the responsibility of commanders and superiors, the United States has failed to hold high-level officials accountable for torture in the present case. In the context of the so-called "war on terror," criminal and military court investigations and trials have taken place *exclusively* against low-ranking members of the military who had been direct participants in the crimes (three low-ranking officers were indeed convicted, but for abuses they committed directly). Twenty cases in which civilian officials, including CIA agents, were accused of abusing detainees have been passed on to the Department of Justice, but there have been no further investigations (with one exception being a case against a private contractor).

While high-ranking officials were not the ones who mistreated detainees with their own hands, were not the ones who waterboarded them, the defendants in this case ordered specific and extremely harsh interrogation techniques, and redefined torture. The language of their orders, requiring soldiers and guards to "take the gloves off," to treat detainees "like dogs" and to "get tough," and their failure to prevent their subordinates from committing crimes or to punish crimes committed, created a climate conducive to further abuse.[29] The fact that the crimes happened in such a widespread and systematic manner makes those at the top of the chain of command responsible for the torture carried on in Iraq, Afghanistan, Guantánamo, and CIA secret prisons.

Scott Horton, who chairs the Committee on International Law of the Association of the Bar of the City of New York, has written about the likelihood that high-ranking officials would be tried in the United States. "I have formed the opinion that no such criminal investigation or prosecution would occur in the near future in the United States for the reason that the criminal investigative and prosecutorial functions are currently controlled by individuals who are involved in the conspiracy to commit war crimes."[30]

Horton particularly criticized the criminal investigations of the abuse at Abu Ghraib for suppressing accounts of abuse and failing to investigate the responsibility of higher-ups:

> MG Fay held group meetings with soldiers in the presence of their group commanding officers. At these meetings, he reminded them that any soldier who had observed the abuse of detainees at Abu Ghraib and other sites and who had failed to report it contemporaneously was guilty of an infraction and could be brought up on charges. He stated that any noncommissioned officer who observed the abuse of detainees at Abu Ghraib and other sites and who failed to intervene or stop it was guilty of an infraction and could be brought up on charges. He then asked if anyone had observed any incidents they wished to discuss with him. The result of such a process is entirely predictable. MG Fay worked hard to limit the number of accounts of abuse in order to sustain a preconceived theory that the abuse at Abu Ghraib was the result of a handful of "rotten apples" rather than systematic instructions rendered through the chain of command. The soldiers with whom I spoke all felt that anyone providing evidence of abuse would be the target of certain retaliation in the form of (i) criminal charges; (ii) hazing and harassment or (iii) potential exposure and "friendly fire" death on the field of battle in Iraq. . . . Soldiers who raised issues about detainee abuse in Iraq were subject to ridicule and threat; one notorious case involved a soldier who, after registering a report of severe abuse, was ordered to be found "mentally deranged," was strapped to a gurney and was flown out of Iraq.[31]

Horton added:

> I consider it noteworthy that the highest profile cases in which the severest sanctions are sought consistently involve those soldiers who through neglect or oversight permitted photographic evidence of the crimes at Abu Ghraib to become public knowledge.

Concerning the Fort Hood court-martials for the Abu Ghraib abuses—prosecuting almost exclusively those seen in the infamous photos—Horton explained how the U.S. judicial authorities were reluctant to have any superior involved in the cases, not even to provide testimony for the defense:

> Defense counsel requested that certain senior officers be immunized so as to compel their testimony (notwithstanding their right against self-incrimination under the U.S. Constitution). The presiding judge, COL James L. Pohl, declined all such requests. It appears quite clear that COL Pohl's motivations in making such rulings included, prominently, protection of the reputation of the armed forces and the integrity of the chain of command.

Only a tiny fraction of the large number implicated has actually been prosecuted. At least six hundred U.S. personnel, mostly military personnel, including at least ten CIA agents and about twenty civilian contractors, are credibly alleged to have been involved in abuse in 330 incidents occurring in Afghanistan, Iraq, and Guantánamo Bay.[32] Incidents include mock executions, shocking a detainee "with an electric transformer," beating and punching detainees sometimes resulting in broken bones, sexual assaults on male and female detainees, homicides, and so on.[33] Some of these incidents were detailed in the Fay-Jones Report.

These cases represent instances of abuse of around 460 separate detainees. Investigations of 260 personnel alleged to have been involved in the abuse have ended in closure of the investigation or findings that have not been reported. Fifty-seven personnel were subjected to administrative discipline, which is less severe than what can be obtained in court-martial. As of July 2007, 79 military personnel are known to have been recommended for court-martial, 10 of which are still pending, and 5 of which resulted in charges being dropped. Although 54 (85 percent) of the remaining 64 resulted in guilty verdicts, only 10 personnel have ultimately faced sentences longer than one year.

And the limited accountability has not risen to the top: 95 percent of the court-martials have involved enlisted personnel, not officers. There is no evidence that officers have been charged for the actions of their subordinates.

Even retired military officials have criticized the lack of prosecution: John H. Johns, Brigadier General, USA (Ret.) has argued that "[f]ocusing on lower level soldiers ignores the role of the systematic climate established by official policy, and the apparent acquiescence by the chain of command. . . . The entire process, from the Department of Justice to the senior officials in the field, circumvented international protocols as well as federal laws on the treatment of prisoners. . . . The behavior of these senior officials represents more serious violations than those at the end of the process. To exonerate them is inexcusable."[34]

The documents in this section all speak to the issue of command responsibility, and range from the statements and testimony of commanders in Washington and in Iraq to excerpts from two reports prepared by investigation teams looking into charges of abuse and torture.

Testimony of General Janis Karpinski

The following excerpts come from testimony by U.S. Army Colonel Janis Karpinski, the commander of the Abu Ghraib prison in 2003, submitted as part of the 2005 German complaint against Donald Rumsfeld.

Colonel Karpinski was demoted from Brigadier General after the torture at Abu Ghraib became public, and she became the military's scapegoat for torture and abuse. Her testimony speaks of who ultimately is responsible for the human rights violations at Abu Ghraib.

The problems at Abu Ghraib started during MG Miller's visit and grew worse with the arrival of the contract interrogators. I would eventually be held responsible for the abuses and the misconduct of the soldiers in the photographs.

The Visit of General Miller: August 31, 2003, to September 9, 2003

General Miller was sent to visit Iraq by Secretary Rumsfeld and the Undersecretary of Defense for Intelligence, Stephen Cambone. MG Miller was serving as the commander of detention operations at Guantánamo Bay, Cuba, and was responsible for . . . beatings, sleep deprivation, solitary confinement, using attack dogs to intimidate prisoners, and other abuses at Guantánamo. He was sent to Abu Ghraib to assist the military intelligence interrogators with enhancing their techniques to obtain more actionable intelligence.

MG Miller conducted an introductory briefing, and I was invited to attend. He planned to visit Abu Ghraib and several other prison facilities to determine what facility he was going to use for interrogations. MG Miller was working almost exclusively with the military intelligence people and the military intelligence interrogators during the course of his visit. He was not interested in assisting with detention operations; rather he was focusing on interrogation operations and teaching interrogators harsher techniques as a means to obtain more actionable intelligence.

MG Miller was spending almost all of his time with the Military Intelligence Officer (J2) BG Barbara Fast and the Commander of the Military Intelligence Brigade, Colonel Pappas. During his in-brief, his introduction when he first arrived there with his team, he responded to a military interrogator's question. This military intelligence interrogator was fairly senior in rank and probably has more than 10 or 12 years of experience because his rank was of a more senior, experienced military person. He was listening to the in-brief and particularly some of MG Miller's comments; the criticisms concerning how the interrogators were conducting the interviews and they were not obtaining really valuable information, so he was there to assist them with different techniques, techniques resulting in more actionable intelligence.

This interrogator just asked the question about what he would recommend they might do immediately to improve their procedures because he thought that they were doing a pretty good job with identifying the people who may have additional value or more military intelligence value.

The interrogator said, "Sir, we think we're doing a good job, it's not like we don't know what we're doing in interrogations, we do have experience." Then MG Miller said, "My first observation is you are not in charge of the interrogations." He said they were being too nice to the prisoners. MG Miller said that the interrogators were not being aggressive enough. He used an example from Guantánamo Bay. He said when the prisoners are brought in, they are always handled by two military policemen and they are escorted *everywhere* they go with leg irons, hand irons and belly chains. He said the prisoners know who is in charge, and then he said, "Look, you have to treat them like dogs. If they ever feel like anything more than dogs, you have effectively lost control of the interrogation." The prisoners at Guantánamo always understood who was in control, according to MG Miller.

He said, "They have to know that you are in charge, and if you treat them too nicely, they will not cooperate with you. At Guantánamo, the prisoners earn every single thing they get, including a change of color of their jumpsuits. When they get there, they're issued a bright orange jumpsuit. They're handled in a very aggressive, forceful manner, and they earn the privilege of transitioning to a white jumpsuit, if they prove themselves to be cooperative." To treat the prisoners like dogs seems to be consistent with those photographs with the dog collar, the dog leash, and un-muzzled dogs. The use of those techniques are mentioned in several memorandums and signed by him, authorizing the use of dogs, even unmuzzled dogs in interrogation operations.

And at this point, I had to raise my hand to respond to his comments. I was just there as a guest, not as a participant, but I said, "You know, sir, the MPs here don't move prisoners with leg irons and hand irons. We don't even have the equipment. We don't have enough funding to buy one jumpsuit per prisoner, let alone an exchange of colors." And he said, "It's no problem. My budget is $125 million a year at Guantánamo, and I'm going to give Colonel Pappas all of the resources he needs to do this appropriately."

It is true Colonel Pappas ran the interrogation operations within the prison. Cell Block 1A and 1B were the only two maximum security wings of the hard site, and during General Miller's visit, either at his order or at his request, General Miller instructed or ordered, Colonel Pappas to "get control" of Cell Block 1A.

MG Miller ultimately selected Abu Ghraib to be the focus of his efforts, and he told me that he was going to make Abu Ghraib "the interrogation center for all of Iraq"; he was going to "Gitmoize" the operation and planned to use the MPs to assist the interrogators by setting the conditions for effective interrogations to take place. His plans required the MPs to enhance interrogations and to obtain more actionable intelligence. I explained to him the MPs were not trained in any kind of inter-rogation operations, but MG Miller told me not to worry because he was going to give them "all the training they needed to do this job" and that he was going to leave the training materials on several compact discs with Colonel Pappas "to make sure the MPs received the right training." MG Miller told me he wanted me "to give him Abu Ghraib" because it was the location he se-lected. I told MG Miller Abu Ghraib was not mine to give him, we only ran detention operations there. MG Miller said, "Look, Rick Sanchez said I could have any facility I wanted and I want Abu Ghraib." He further stated, "Look, we can do this my way or we can do this the hard way," as if we were on opposite sides from each other.

My First Knowledge of the Photographs

I was first informed of the situation at Abu Ghraib and "the on-going investigation" by an email I received in classified—what is called "classified traffic." I opened it up late one night on January 12, 2004. It was from the commander of the Criminal Investiga-tion Division. He sent me an email and said, "Ma'am, I just want to make you aware, I'm going in to brief the CG," meaning Gen-eral Sanchez, "on the progress of the investigation at Abu Ghraib. This involves the allegations of abuse and the photographs." This was the first I heard anything about any investigation or any-thing about abuses or anything about photographs.

I did not receive an email or even so much as a telephone call or a message from General Sanchez himself, who would ulti-mately attempt to hold me fully responsible for this. I was alarmed with just the information in the short email, and I was not in Baghdad at the time. I was at another location very close to the Iranian border, so we made arrangements to leave at the crack of dawn to drive down to Abu Ghraib to see what we could find out about this "ongoing investigation."

The Sergeant pointed out a memo posted on a column just outside of their small administrative office. The memorandum was signed by the Secretary of Defense, Donald Rumsfeld, and it discussed Authorized Interrogation techniques including use of loud music and prolonged standing positions, amongst several other techniques. It was one page. It mentioned stress positions, noise and light discipline, the use of music, disrupting sleep patterns, those types of techniques. There was also a handwritten note out to the side in the same ink and in the same script as the signature of the Secretary of Defense. The notation written in the margin said "Make sure this happens!" This memorandum was a copy; a photocopy of the original, I would imagine. I thought it was unusual for an interrogation memorandum to be posted inside of a detention cell block, because interrogations were not conducted in the cell block, at least to my understanding and knowledge. Interrogations were conducted in one of the two interrogation facilities outside of the hard site.

This was the command of Donald Rumsfeld himself talking about the specific interrogation techniques he was authorizing. And there was the note—the handwritten note out to the side. It said, "Make sure this happens." And it seemed to be in the same handwriting as the signature. And people understood it to be from Rumsfeld. This is all of what I can say about the memorandum.

Contributing Factors

I believe many of the contributing factors, blurring of the lines of command, conflicting missions, no oversight, transferring the Prison Facility to the control of a Military Intelligence Officer, etc., were intentionally designed to cause confusion at Abu Ghraib.

MG Miller made the statement concerning his plans for Abu Ghraib, "I am going to make Abu Ghraib the Interrogation Center for all of Iraq." This is, in reality, what happened over the course of two months time. Although MG Miller testified before the U.S. Senate Armed Services Committee, saying he had no authority in Iraq so it was impossible for anyone to accuse him of directing any operations relative to Abu Ghraib or interrogations, it was later proven that he exercised wide reaching authority from Guantánamo concerning both the operations at Abu Ghraib and interrogation operations at Abu Ghraib and other locations where interrogations were conducted. He was in daily discussions and communications via emails with Sanchez, Fast, and Pappas concerning the results and effectiveness of the interrogation techniques implemented during his visit. Sanchez, Fast, and Pappas provided daily reports to MG Miller concerning information derived from interrogations.

Donald Rumsfeld came to visit, and I expressed my concerns about the conditions in the prisons. I spoke directly to Ambassador Bremer every week. I spoke to General Sanchez at least once every week, reported it in the updates and the night time briefings to General Wodjakowski, the deputy at CJTF-7, about the lack of funding, for even the basic supplies: a basin for washing, a change of clothing, for the prisoners.

After I saw the photographs for the first time, on January 23, only 11 days after I received the only email informing me there was an "ongoing investigation," I tried to find out as much information and ask as many questions as I could, but there were no conversations at all about the details of the photographs, no meeting with General Sanchez, no discussion about this situation at all. I was not able to speak to Colonel Pappas or any one of the soldiers in the photographs. I was told by Col. Warren (JAG for Ltg. Sanchez), "No Ma'am, you cannot see the soldiers. You are not authorized because they do not work for you. They work for Col. Pappas and he is the only Commander authorized to speak to them."

The only person I spoke to individually after General Miller's initial briefing was the JAG Officer who was with General Miller. She was working down at Guantánamo Bay in her last assignment.

Her name was Major Laura Beavers. I asked her, "What are you doing about releasing the prisoners down at Guantánamo Bay?" She said, "Ma'am, we're not releasing prisoners. Most of those prisoners are going to spend every last day of their lives at Guantánamo. They're terrorists. We're not releasing them." I said, "Well, what are you going to do? Fly their family members over to visit them?" She said "No, these are terrorists, ma'am. They don't get visits from home." I remember an image of "no end in sight," guarding prisoners at Guantánamo and in Iraq for an unspecified length of time did not seem like a favorable idea of democracy or anything close to nation building.

Officials To Be Punished
If officials are to be punished, we have to start at the very top, and the original memorandum directing interrogation—harsher interrogation techniques and the departure from the Geneva Conventions starts at the very top, the White House. Alberto Gonzales was one of the people who made the recommendations to the President. I don't know if he talked about each detail of the departure from the Geneva Conventions or what it may imply, but I do know that the Secretary of Defense signed a very lengthy memorandum authorizing harsher techniques to be used in Afghanistan and specifically at Guantánamo Bay. It seems those memorandums would have been made available to me as the Commander of all Detention Operations in Iraq, however I was never made aware of the documents or the authorizations contained in them.

Those techniques migrated from Guantánamo Bay to Iraq during the visit of MG Miller and his Tiger Team and were implemented at Abu Ghraib. Clearly to be punished are the Secretary of Defense, Undersecretary Cambone, his assistant who sent General Miller to Iraq with very specific instructions on how to work with the military intelligence people; General Fast, who was directing interrogation operations and giving instructions to Colonel Pappas on how to proceed and how to be more effective; General Sanchez, because Abu Ghraib was his command, and he knew what General Fast was doing, and he knew what Colonel Pappas was doing, to the point that Colonel Pappas made a comment one time that he thought maybe he had a bruise on his chest because LTG Sanchez repeatedly poked him in the chest telling him to "Get Saddam! Get Saddam!" and directed him (Pappas) to use whatever means he needed to use to get the information.

The lower level soldiers have been unfairly and unjustly held accountable for all of this, as if they designed these techniques, as if Lynndie England deployed with a dog collar and a dog leash. Should they be punished for doing what they did, for agreeing to do what they did? Absolutely. But singled out? No.

Testimony of Lawrence Wilkerson

Colonel Lawrence Wilkerson is the former Chief of Staff to Secretary of State Colin Powell. Prior to his retirement in January 2005, he was a leading critic of President Bush's policies post-9/11. The following quotes from Wilkerson illustrate his belief that it is top officials who are to blame for the program of torture and harsh interrogations post-9/11.

Excerpt from a November 29, 2005, BBC News Report, "Cheney Accused on Prisoner Abuse": "What I'm saying is that, under the vice-president's protection, the secretary of defense [Donald Rumsfeld] moved out to do what they wanted in the first place, even though the president had made a decision that was clearly a compromise," Col Wilkerson said.

He said that he laid the blame on the issue of prisoner abuse and post-war planning for Iraq "pretty fairly and squarely" at Mr Cheney's feet.

"I look at the relationship between Mr Cheney and Mr Rumsfeld as being one that produced these two failures in particular, and I see that the president is not holding either of them accountable . . . so I have to lay some blame at his feet too," he went on.

From a talk at the Neiman Foundation for Journalism at Harvard University, July 11, 2006: There is, in my view, insufficient evidence to walk into an American courtroom and win a legal case (though an international courtroom for war crimes might feel differently). But there is enough evidence for a soldier of long service—someone like me with 31 years in the Army—to know that what started with John Yoo, David Addington, Alberto Gonzales, William Haynes at the Pentagon, and several others, all under the watchful and willing eye of the Vice President, went down through the Secretary of Defense to the commanders in the field, and created two separate pressures that resulted in the violation of longstanding practice and law.

From an article entitled "The Memo" by Jane Mayer, which appeared in the February 27, 2006, issue of the *New Yorker*. The "scrawled aside" refers to Rumsfeld's infamous "I stand" note: Colonel Lawrence Wilkerson, a retired military officer who was a chief of staff to former Secretary of State Colin Powell, had a similar reaction when he saw Rumsfeld's scrawled aside: "It said, 'Carte blanche, guys,'" Wilkerson told me. "That's what started them down the slope. You'll have My Lais then. Once you pull this thread, the whole fabric unravels."

The Schlesinger Report

The following document is an excerpt from the "Independent Panel to Review DoD Detention Operations," commonly known as the Schlesinger Report. The independent panel, led by former Secretary of Defense James R. Schlesinger, was convened by the Pentagon to investigate detainee abuse at Abu Ghraib and recommend solutions. The panel released its report in August 2004. The report confirmed that the entire Pentagon chain of command, including Donald Rumsfeld, was responsible for the torture and abuses at Abu Ghraib. The following excerpts make clear that it was Major General Geoffrey Miller and Donald Rumsfeld whose authorizations led to the abusive tactics used by interrogators at Abu Ghraib.

In August 2003, MG Geoffrey Miller arrived to conduct an assessment of DoD counter-terrorism interrogation and detention operations in Iraq. He was to discuss theater ability to exploit internees rapidly for actionable intelligence. He brought the Secretary of Defense's April 16, 2003, policy guidelines for Guantánamo with him and gave this policy to CJTF-7 as a possible model for the command-wide policy that he recommended be established. MG Miller noted that it applied to unlawful combatants at Guantánamo and was not directly applicable to Iraq where the Geneva Conventions applied.[35] In part as a result of MG Miller's call for strong, command-wide interrogation policies and in part as a result of a request for guidance coming up from the 519th at Abu Ghraib, on September 14, 2003, LTG Sanchez signed a memorandum authorizing a dozen interrogation techniques beyond Field Manual 34-52—five beyond those approved for Guantánamo.

Although specifically limited by the Secretary of Defense to Guantánamo, and requiring his personal approval (given in only two cases), the augmented techniques for Guantánamo migrated to Afghanistan and Iraq where they were neither limited nor safeguarded.

It is clear that pressure for additional intelligence and the more aggressive methods sanctioned by the Secretary of Defense memorandum resulted in stronger interrogation techniques.

[T]he Independent Panel finds that commanding officers and their staffs at various levels failed in their duties and that such failures contributed directly or indirectly to detainee abuse. Commanders are responsible for all their units do or fail to do, and should be held accountable for their action or inaction. Command failures were compounded by poor advice provided by staff officers with responsibility for overseeing battlefield functions related to detention and interrogation operations. Military and civilian leaders at the Department of Defense share this burden of responsibility."

The Fay-Jones Report

The following excerpt is from a third report focusing on detainee abuse and torture at Abu Ghraib by the 205th Military Intelligence Brigade, which was in charge of the prison. A Pentagon internal inquiry into the abuse at Abu Ghraib, led by Major Gen. George Fay and Lt. Gen. Anthony Jones, released a 177-page report in August 2004. The report's authors laid the blame for abuse at the feet of Commander Ricardo Sanchez and his deputies, the top commanders at Abu Ghraib, including Col. Thomas Pappas. In these excerpts, CJTF-7 refers to the Combined Joint Task Force 7, which encompassed all U.S. armed forces in Iraq and was commanded by Sanchez.

The chain of command directly above the 205th MI Brigade was not directly involved in the abuses at Abu Ghraib. However, policy memoranda promulgated by the CJTF-7 Commander led indirectly to some of the non-violent and non-sexual abuses. In addition, the CJTF-7 Commander and Deputy Commander failed to ensure proper staff oversight of detention and interrogation operations. Finally, CJTF-7 staff elements reacted inadequately to earlier indications and warnings that problems existed at Abu Ghraib.

The policy memos promulgated at the CJTF-7 level allowed for interpretation in several areas, including use of dogs and removal of clothing. Particularly, in light of the wide spectrum of interrogator qualifications, maturity, and experiences (i.e. in GTMO and Afghanistan), the memos did not adequately set forth the limits on interrogation techniques.

Individual Responsibility for Detainee Abuse at Abu Ghraib
Finding: COL Thomas M. Pappas, Commander, 205 MI BDE. A preponderance of evidence supports that COL Pappas did, or failed to do, the following:

- Failed to insure that the JIDC[36] performed its mission to its full capabilities, within the applicable rules, regulations and appropriate procedures.

- Failed to properly organize the JIDC.
- Failed to put the necessary checks and balances in place to prevent and detect abuses.
- Failed to ensure that his Soldiers and civilians were properly trained for the mission.
- Showed poor judgment by leaving LTC Jordan in charge of the JIDC during the critical early stages of the JIDC.
- Showed poor judgment by leaving LTC Jordan in charge during the aftermath of a shooting incident known as the Iraqi Police Roundup (IP Roundup).
- Improperly authorized the use of dogs during interrogations. Failed to properly supervise the use of dogs to make sure they were muzzled after he improperly permitted their use.
- Failed to take appropriate action regarding the ICRC reports of abuse.
- Failed to take aggressive action against Soldiers who violated . . . the CJTF-7 Interrogation and Counter-Resistance Policy and the Geneva Conventions.
- Failed to properly communicate to Higher Headquarters when his Brigade would be unable to accomplish its mission due to lack of manpower and/or resources. Allowed his Soldiers and civilians at the JIDC to be subjected to inordinate pressure from Higher Headquarters.
- Failed to establish appropriate MI and MP coordination at the brigade level which would have alleviated much of the confusion that contributed to the abusive environment at Abu Ghraib.
- The significant number of systemic failures documented in this report does not relieve COL Pappas of his responsibility as the Commander, 205th MI BDE for the abuses that occurred and went undetected for a considerable length of time.

4

Witnesses and Statements for the Defense

In this section, you will read the evidence the defendants have put forth to justify their program of torture and abuse. This evidence includes public statements, testimony, and documentary evidence such as memos explaining why the defendants believe harsh interrogation tactics are, in fact, legal. Most of these memos were initially classified, but many have since been leaked to the press. In the materials that follow, the defendants argue both that the Geneva Conventions are inapplicable and that the interrogation methods that were employed did not constitute torture and were necessary to prevent the next terrorist act.

Donald Rumsfeld Public Statements

In a January 11, 2002, Reuters article, Donald Rumsfeld makes the distinction for the first time between calling the Guantánamo detainees "enemy combatants" and calling them "prisoners of war." Enemy combatants are technically not covered by the Geneva Conventions, allowing the administration to argue that Geneva's protections against torture do not apply to such detainees.

" '[The Guantánamo detainees] will be handled not as prisoners of war, because they are not, but as unlawful combatants,' Rumsfeld said in response to questions."

" 'Technically, unlawful combatants do not have any rights under the Geneva convention. We have indicated that we do plan to, for the most part, treat them in a manner that is reasonably consistent with the Geneva conventions to the extent they are appropriate,' Rumsfeld said."[1]

In a February 7, 2002, transcript of a speech at a Joint Strike Fighter Signing Ceremony, Rumsfeld contends that the conditions of the present conflict with al Qaeda and the Taliban make the Geneva Conventions somewhat anachronistic.

"But the reality is that the set of facts that exist today with respect to al Qaeda and Taliban were not necessarily the kinds of facts that were considered when the Geneva Convention was fashioned some half a century ago."[2]

Defense Memos

The following memo by the attorneys among the defendants lays out the defendants' arguments supporting the interrogation methods employed by the U.S. government post-9/11. These memos form the legal framework that other defendants, such as Donald Rumsfeld, point to as the justification for their torture and interrogation policies.

Many of the legal arguments flowed from the Office of Legal Counsel (OLC), located within the Department of Justice. Headed at the time by Jay Bybee, the OLC drafts the attorney general's legal opinions and also drafts its own opinions in response to requests from various executive branch agencies. The OLC is also responsible for giving the president legal advice on issues of constitutionality. Importantly, the legal reasoning of the Office of Legal Counsel becomes, essentially, the law.

John Yoo worked under Bybee at the OLC and helped draft many of the memos. Gonzales, as the White House counsel, acted with the authority of the President and had the ability to override the legal opinions of Bybee and Yoo. Delahunty was deputy legal counsel to the president and reported to Gonzales. Haynes was at the Pentagon and advised Rumsfeld on legal issues.

January 9, 2002, John Yoo

In this memo, John Yoo, then-deputy assistant attorney general, reporting to Jay Bybee, assistant attorney general, states his view that the Geneva Conventions do not apply to captured Taliban or al Qaeda fighters. He further argues that international laws do not apply to the United States, because international laws do not have any status under U.S. federal law. According to the logic of this memo, the discretion of the U.S. president determines whether the country will follow any precept of international law when it comes to the detention and trial of members of the Taliban or al Qaeda. Yoo prepared the memo for William Haynes; this memo forms the legal basis for much of the Bush administration's arguments regarding issues including detention and torture.

U.S. Department of Justice
Office of Legal Counsel

Office of the Deputy Assistant Attorney General   Washington D.C. 20530
January 9, 2002

MEMORANDUM FOR WILLIAM J. HAYNES II
   GENERAL COUNSEL, DEPARTMENT OF DEFENSE

FROM: John Yoo   DRAFT
         Deputy Assistant Attorney General

         Robert J. Delahunty
         'Special Counsel'

RE: *Application of Treaties and Laws to al Qaeda and Taliban Detainees*

You have asked for our Office's views concerning the effect of international treaties and federal laws on the treatment of individuals detained by the U.S. Armed Forces during the conflict in Afghanistan. In particular, you have asked whether the laws of armed conflict apply to the conditions of detention and the procedures for trial of members of al Qaeda and the Taliban militia. We conclude that these treaties do not protect members of the al Qaeda organization, which as a non-State actor cannot be a party to the international agreements governing war. We further conclude that that these treaties do not apply to the Taliban militia. This memorandum expresses no view as to whether the President should decide, as a matter of policy, that the U.S. Armed Forces should adhere to the standards of conduct in those treaties with respect to the treatment of prisoners.

We believe it most useful to structure the analysis of these questions by focusing on the War Crimes Act, 18 U.S.C. § 2441 (Supp. III 1997) ("WCA"). The WCA directly incorporates several provisions of international treaties governing the laws of war into the federal criminal code. Part I of this memorandum describes the WCA and the most relevant treaties that it incorporates: the four 1949 Geneva Conventions, which generally regulate the treatment of non-combatants, such as prisoners of war ("POWs"), the injured and sick, and civilians.[1]

Part II examines whether al Qaeda detainees can claim the protections of these agreements. Al Qaeda is merely a violent political movement or organization and not a nation-state. As a result, it is ineligible to be a signatory to any treaty. Because of the novel nature of this conflict, moreover, we do not believe that al

---

[1] The four Geneva Conventions for the Protection of Victims of War, dated August 12, 1949, were ratified by the United States on July 14, 1955. These are the Convention for the Amelioration of the Condition of the Wounded and Sick in Armed Forces in the Field, 6 U.S.T. 3115 ("Geneva Convention I"); the Convention for the Amelioration of the Condition of Wounded, Sick and Shipwrecked Members of Armed Forces at Sea, 6 U.S.T. 3219 ("Geneva Convention II"); the Convention Relative to the Treatment of Prisoners of War, 6 U.S.T. 3517 ("Geneva Convention III"); and the Convention Relative to the Protection of Civilian Persons in Time of War, 6 U.S.T. 3317 ("Geneva Convention IV").

Qaeda would be included in non-international forms of armed conflict to which some provisions of the Geneva Conventions might apply. Therefore, neither the Geneva Conventions nor the WCA regulate the detention of al Qaeda prisoners captured during the Afghanistan conflict.

Part III discusses whether the same treaty provisions, as incorporated through the WCA, apply to the treatment of captured members of the Taliban militia. We believe that the Geneva Conventions do not apply for several reasons. First, the Taliban was not a government and Afghanistan was not—even prior to the beginning of the present conflict—a functioning State during the period in which they engaged in hostilities against the United States and its allies. Afghanistan's status as a failed state is ground alone to find that members of the Taliban militia are not entitled to enemy POW status under the Geneva Conventions. Further, it is clear that the President has the constitutional authority to suspend our treaties with Afghanistan pending the restoration of a legitimate government capable of performing Afghanistan's treaty obligations. Second, it appears from the public evidence that the Taliban militia may have been so intertwined with al Qaeda as to be functionally indistinguishable from it. To the extent that the Taliban militia was more akin to a non-governmental organization that used military force to pursue its religious and political ideology than a functioning government, its members would be on the same legal footing as al Qaeda.

In Part IV, we address the question whether any customary international law of armed conflict might apply to the al Qaeda or Taliban militia members detained during the course of the Afghanistan conflict. We conclude that customary international law, whatever its source and content, does not bind the President, or restrict the actions of the United States military, because it does not constitute federal law recognized under the Supremacy Clause of the Constitution. The President, however, has the constitutional authority as Commander in Chief to interpret and apply the customary or common laws of war in such a way that they would extend to the conduct of members of both al Qaeda and the Taliban, and also to the conduct of the U.S. Armed Forces towards members of those groups taken as prisoners in Afghanistan.

I. Background and Overview of the War Crimes Act and the Geneva Conventions

It is our understanding that your Department is considering two basic plans regarding the treatment of members of al Qaeda and the Taliban militia detained during the Afghanistan conflict. First, the Defense Department intends to make available a facility at the U.S. Navy base at Guantanamo Bay, Cuba, for the long-term detention of these individuals, who have come under our control either through capture by our military or transfer from our allies in Afghanistan. We have discussed in a separate memorandum the federal jurisdiction issues that might arise concerning Guantanamo Bay.[2] Second, your Department is developing procedures to implement the President's Military Order of November 13, 2001, which establishes military commissions for the trial of violations of the laws of war committed by non-U.S. citizens.[3] The question has arisen whether the Geneva Conventions, or other relevant international treaties or federal laws, regulate these proposed policies.

[2] *See* Memorandum for William J. Haynes II, General Counsel, Department of Defense, from: Patrick F. Philbin, Deputy Assistant Attorney General, and John Yoo, Deputy Assistant Attorney General, *Re: Possible Habeas Jurisdiction over Aliens Held in Guantanamo Bay, Cuba* (Dec. 28, 2001).

[3] *See generally* Memorandum for Alberto R. Gonzales, Counsel to the President, from Patrick F. Philbin, Deputy Assistant Attorney General, Office of Legal Counsel, *Re: Legality of the Use of Military Commissions to Try Terrorists* (Nov. 6, 2001).

We believe that the WCA provides a useful starting point for our analysis of the application of the Geneva Conventions to the treatment of detainees captured in the Afghanistan theater of operations.[4] Section 2441 of Title 18 renders certain acts punishable as "war crimes." The statute's definition of that term incorporates, by reference, certain treaties or treaty provisions relating to the laws of war, including the Geneva Conventions.

A. Section 2441: An Overview

Section 2441 reads in full as follows:

War crimes

(a) Offense.-Whoever, whether inside or outside the United States, commits a war crime, in any of the circumstances described in subsection (b), shall be fined under this title or imprisoned for life or any term of years, or both, and if death results to the victim, shall also be subject to the penalty of death.

(b) Circumstances.-The circumstances referred to in subsection (a) are that the person committing such war crime or the victim of such war crime is a member of the Armed Forces of the United States or a national of the United States (as defined in section 101 of the Immigration and Nationality Act).

(c) Definition.–As used in this section the term "war crime" means any conduct–

---

[4] The rule of lenity requires that the WCA be read to as to ensure that prospective defendants have adequate notice of the nature of the acts that the statute condemns. *See, e.g., Castillo v. United States,* 530 U.S. 120, 131 (2000). In those cases in which the application of a treaty incorporated by the WCA is unclear, therefore, the rule of lenity requires that the interpretative issue be resolved in the defendant's favor.

(1) defined as a grave breach in any of the international conventions signed at Geneva 12 August 1949, or any protocol to such convention to which the United States is a party;

(2) prohibited by Article 23, 25, 27, or 28 of the Annex to the Hague Convention IV, Respecting the Laws and Customs of War on Land, signed 18 October 1907;

(3) which constitutes a violation of common Article 3 of the international conventions signed at Geneva, 12 August 1949, or any protocol to such convention to which the United States is a party and which deals with non-international armed conflict; or

(4) of a person who, in relation to an armed conflict and contrary to the provisions of the Protocol on Prohibitions or Restrictions on the Use of Mines, Booby-Traps and Other Devices as amended at Geneva on 3 May 1996 (Protocol II as amended on 3 May 1996), when the United States is a party to such Protocol, willfully kills or causes serious injury to civilians.

18 U.S.C. § 2441

Section 2441 lists four categories of war crimes. First, it criminalizes "grave breaches" of the Geneva Conventions, which are defined by treaty and will be discussed below. Second, it makes illegal conduct prohibited by articles 23, 25, 27 and 28 of the Annex to the Hague Convention IV. Third, it criminalizes violations of what is known as "common" Article 3, which is an identical provision common to all four of the Geneva Conventions. Fourth, it criminalizes conduct prohibited by certain other laws of war treaties, once the United States joins them. A House Report states that the original legislation "carries out the international obligations of the United States under the Geneva Conventions of 1949 to provide criminal penalties for certain war crimes." H.R. Rep. No. 104–698 at 1 (1996), *reprinted in* 1996 U.S.C.C.A.N. 2166, 2166. Each of those four conventions includes a clause relating to legislative implementation and to criminal punishment.[5]

In enacting section 2441, Congress also sought to fill certain perceived gaps in the coverage of federal criminal law. The main gaps were thought to be of two kinds: subject matter jurisdiction and personal jurisdiction. First, Congress found that "[t]here are major gaps in the prosecutability of individuals under federal criminal law for war crimes committed against Americans." H.R. Rep. No. 104–698 at 6, *reprinted in* 1996 U.S.C.C.A.N. at 2171. For example, "the simple killing of a[n American] prisoner of war" was not covered by any existing Federal statute. *Id.* at 5, *reprinted in* 1996 U.S.C.C.A.N. at 2170.[6] Second, Congress found that "[t]he ability

---

[5] That common clause reads as follows:

> The [signatory Nations] undertake to exact any legislation necessary to provide effective penal sanctions for persons committing, or ordering to be committed, any of the grave breaches of the present Convention. . . . Each [signatory nation] shall be under the obligation to search for persons alleged to have committed, or to have ordered to be committed, such grave breaches, and shall bring such persons, regardless of their nationality, before its own courts. . . . It may also, if it prefers, . . . hand such persons over for trial to another [signatory nation], provided such [nation] has made out a *prima facic* case.

Geneva Convention I, art. 49; Geneva Convention II, art. 50; Geneva Convention III, art. 129; Geneva Convention IV, art. 146.

[6] In projecting our criminal law extraterritorially in order to protect victims who are United States nationals, Congress was apparently relying on the international law principle of passive personality. The passive personality principle "asserts that a state may apply law—particularly criminal law—to an act committed outside its territory by a person not its national where the victim of the act was its national." *United States v.*

to court martial members of our armed services who commit war crimes ends when they leave military service. [Section 2441] would allow for prosecution even after discharge." *Id.* at 7, *reprinted in* 1996 U.S.C.C.A.N. at 2172.[7] Congress considered it important to fill this gap, not only in the interest of the victims of war crimes, but also of the accused. "The Americans prosecuted would have available all the procedural protections of the American justice system. These might be lacking if the United States extradited the individuals to their victims' home countries for prosecution." *Id.*[8] Accordingly, Section 2441 criminalizes forms of conduct in which a U.S. national or a member of the Armed Forces may be either a victim or a perpetrator.

B. Grave Breaches of the Geneva Conventions

The Geneva Conventions were approved by a diplomatic conference on August 12, 1949, and remain the agreements to which more States have become parties than any other concerning the laws of war. Convention I deals with the treatment of wounded

---

Recap, 134 F.3d 1121, 1133 (D.C. Cir.). *cert. denied,* 525 U.S. 834 (1998). The principle marks recognition of the fact that "each nation has a legitimate interest that its nationals and permanent inhabitants not be maimed or disabled from self-support," or otherwise injured. *Louritsen v. Lorsen,* 345 U.S. 571, 586 (1953): *see also Hellenic Lines Ltd. v. Rhoditis,* 398 U.S. 306, 309 (1970).

[7] In *United States ex rel. Toth v. Quarles,* 350 U.S. 11 (1955), the Supreme Court had held that a former serviceman could not constitutionally be tried before a court martial under the Uniform Code for Military Justice (the "UCMJ") for crimes be was alleged to have committed while in the armed services.

[8] The principle of nationality in international law recognizes that (as Congress did here) a State may criminalize acts performed extraterritorially by its own nationals. *See e.g. Shriotes v. Florida,* 313 U.S. 69, 73 (1941); *Steele v. Bulova Watch Co.,* 344 U.S. 280, 282 (1952).

and sick in armed forces in the field; Convention II addresses treatment of the wounded, sick, and shipwrecked in armed forces at sea; Convention III regulates treatment of POWs; Convention IV addresses the treatment of citizens. While the Hague Convention IV establishes the rules of conduct against the enemy, the Geneva Conventions set the rules for the treatment of the victims of war.

The Geneva Conventions, like treaties generally, structure legal relationships between Nation States, not between Nation States and private, subnational groups or organizations.[9] All four Conventions share the same Article 2, known as "common Article 2." It states:

In addition to the provisions which shall be implemented in peacetime, the present Convention shall apply to all cases of declared war or of any other armed conflict *which may arise between two or more of the High Contracting Parties,* even if the state of war is not recognized by one of them.

The Convention shall also apply to all cases of partial or total occupation of the territory of a High Contracting Party, even if the said occupation meets with no armed resistance.

Although one of the Powers in conflict may not be a party to the present Convention, the Powers who are par-

---

[9] *See Trans World Airlines, Inc. v. Franklin Mint Corp.,* 466 U.S. 243, 253 (1984) ("A treaty is in the nature of a contract between nations."), *The Head Money Cases,* 112 U.S. 580, 598 (1884) ("A treaty is primarily a compact between independent nations."); *United States ex rel. Saroop v. Garcia,* 109 F3d 165, 167 (3d Cir. 1997) ("[T]reaties are agreements between nations."); *Vienna Convention on the Law of Treaties,* May 23, 1969, art. 2, § 1(a), 1155 U.N.T.S. 331, 333 ("[T]reaty' means an international agreement concluded between States in written form and governed by international law. . . .") (the "Vienna Convention"); *see generally Banco Naçional de Cuba v. Sabbatino,* 376 U.S. 398, 422 (1964) ("The traditional view of international law is that it establishes substantive principles for determining whether one country has wronged another.").

ties thereto shall remain bound by it in their mutual relations. They shall furthermore be bound by the Convention in relation to the said Power, if the latter accepts and applies the provisions thereof.

(Emphasis added).

As incorporated by § 2441(c)(1), the four Geneva Conventions similarly define "grave breaches." Geneva Convention III on POWs defines a grave breach as:

wilful killing, torture or inhuman treatment, including biological experiments, wilfully causing great suffering or serious injury to body or health, compelling a prisoner of war to serve in the forces of the hostile Power, or wilfully depriving a prisoner of war of the rights of fair and regular trial prescribed in this Convention.

Geneva Convention III, art. 130. As mentioned before, the Geneva Conventions require the High Contracting Parties to enact penal legislation to punish anyone who commits or orders a grave breach: *See, e.g., id.* art. 129. Further, each State party has the obligation to search for and bring to justice (either before its courts or by delivering a suspect to another State party) anyone who commits a grave breach. No State party is permitted to absolve itself or any other nation of liability for committing a grave breach.

Thus, the WCA does not criminalize all breaches of the Geneva Conventions. Failure to follow some of the regulations regarding the treatment of POWs, such as difficulty in meeting all of the conditions set forth for POW camp conditions, does not constitute a grave breach within the meaning of Geneva Convention III, art. 130. Only by causing great suffering or serious bodily injury to POWs, killing or torturing them, depriving them of access to a fair trial, or forcing them to serve in the Armed Forces, could the United States actually commit a grave breach. Similarly, unintentional, isolated collateral damage on civilian targets would not constitute a grave breach within the meaning of Geneva Convention IV, art. 147. Article 147 requires that for a grave breach to have occurred, destruction of property must have been done "wantonly" and without military justification, while the killing or injury of civilians must have been "wilful."

D. *Common Article 3 of the Geneva Conventions*

Section 2441(c)(3) also defines as a war crime conduct that "constitutes a violation of common Article 3" of the Geneva Conventions. Article 3 is a unique provision that governs the conduct of signatories to the Conventions in a particular kind of conflict that is *not* one between High Contracting Parties to the Conventions. Thus, common Article 3 may require the United States, as a High Contracting Party, to follow certain rules even if other parties to the conflict are not parties to the Conventions. On the other hand. Article 3 requires state parties to follow only certain minimum standards of treatment toward prisoners, civilians, or the sick and wounded, rather than the Conventions as a whole.

Common Article 3 reads in relevant part as follows:

In the case of armed conflict not of an international character occurring in the territory of one of the High Contracting Parties, each Party to the conflict shall be bound to apply, as a minimum, the following provisions:

(1) Persons taking no active part in the hostilities, including members of armed forces who have laid down their arms and those placed *hors de combat* by sickness, wounds, detention, or any other cause, shall in all circumstances be treated humanely, without any adverse distinction founded on race, color, religion or faith, sex, birth or wealth, or any other similar criteria.

To this end, the following acts are and shall remain prohibited at any time and in any place whatsoever with respect to the above-mentioned persons:

(a) violence to life and person, in particular murder of all kinds, mutilation, cruel treatment and torture;

(b) taking of hostages;

(c) outrages upon personal dignity, in particular humiliating and degrading treatment;

(d) the passing of sentences and the carrying out of executions without previous judgment pronounced by a regularly constituted court, affording all the judicial guarantees which are recognized as indispensable by civilized peoples.

(2) The wounded and sick shall be collected and cared for. . . .

The application of the preceding provisions shall not affect the legal status of the Parties to the conflict.

Common article 3 complements common Article 2. Article 2 applies to cases of declared war or of any other armed conflict that may arise between two or more of the High Contracting Parties, even if the state of war is not recognized by one of them.[10] Common Article 3, however, covers "armed conflict not of an international character"—a war that does not involve cross-border attacks—that occurs within the territory of one of the High Contracting Parties. There is substantial reason to think that this language refers specifically to a condition of civil war, or a large-scale

---

[10] Article 2's reference to a state of war "not recognized" by a belligerent was apparently intended to refer to conflicts such as the 1937 war between China and Japan. Both sides denied that a state of war existed. *See* Joyce A. C. Gotteridge, *The Geneva Conventions of 1949,* 26 Brit. Y.B. Int'l L. 294, 298–99 (1949).

armed conflict between a State and an armed movement within its own territory.

To begin with, Article 3's text strongly supports the interpretation that it applies to large-scale conflicts between a State and an insurgent group. First, the language at the end of Article 3 states that "[t]he application of the preceding provisions shall not affect the legal status of the Parties to the conflict." This provision was designed to ensure that a Party that observed Article 3 during a civil war would not be understood to have granted the "recognition of the insurgents as an adverse party." Frits Kalshoven, *Constraints on the Waging of War* 59 (1987). Second, Article 3 is in terms limited to "armed conflict . . . occurring *in the territory of one of the High Contracting Parties*" (emphasis added). This limitation makes perfect sense if the Article applies to civil wars, which are fought primarily or solely within the territory of a single state. The limitation makes little sense, however, as applied to a conflict between a State and a transnational terrorist group, which may operate from different territorial bases, some of which might be located in States that are parties to the Conventions and some of which might not be. In such a case, the Conventions would apply to a single armed conflict in some scenes of action but not in others—which seems inexplicable.

This interpretation is supported by commentators. One well-known commentary states that "a non-international armed conflict is distinct from an international armed conflict because of the legal status of the entities opposing each other: the parties to the conflict are not sovereign States, but the government of a single State in conflict with one or more armed factions within its territory."[11] A legal scholar writing in the same year in which the Conventions were prepared stated that "a conflict not of an inter-

---

[11] Commentary on the Additional Protocols of 3 June 1977 to the Geneva Conventions of 12 August 1949, at ¶ 4339 (Yves Sandoz et al. eds., 1987)

national character occurring in the territory of one of the High Contracting Parties . . . must normally mean a civil war."[12]

Analysis of the background to the adoption of the Geneva Conventions in 1949 confirms our understanding of common Article 3. It appears that the drafters of the Conventions had in mind only the two forms of armed conflict that were regarded as matters of general *international* concern at the time: armed conflict between Nation States (subject to Article 2), and large-scale civil war within a Nation State (subject to Article 3). To understand the context in which the Geneva Conventions were drafted, it will be helpful to identify three distinct phases in the development of the laws of war.

First, the traditional law of war was based on a stark dichotomy between "belligerency" and "insurgency." The category of "belligerency" applied to armed conflicts between sovereign States (unless there was recognition of belligerency in a civil war), while the category of "insurgency" applied to armed violence breaking out within the territory of a sovereign State.[13] Correspondingly, international law treated the two classes of conflict in different ways. Interstate wars were regulated by a body of international legal rules governing both the conduct of hostilities and the protection of noncombatants. By contrast, there were very few international rules governing civil unrest, for States preferred to regard internal strife as rebellion, mutiny and treason coming within the purview of national criminal law, which precluded any possible intrusion by other States.[14]

[12] Gutteridge, *supra* n.10, at 300.

[13] *See* Joseph H. Beale, Jr., *The Recognition of Cuban Belligerency,* 9 Harv. L. Rev. 406, 406 n.1 (1896).

[14] *See The Prosecutor v. Duslco Tadic (Jurisdiction of the Tribunal),* (Appeals Chamber of the International Criminal Tribunal for the Former Yugoslavia 1995) (the "ICTY"), 105 I.I.R. 453, 504–05 (E. Lamerpacht and C.J. Greenwood eds., 1997).

This was a "clearly sovereignty-oriented" phase of international law.[15]

The second phase began as early as the Spanish Civil War (1936–39) and extended through the time of the drafting of the Geneva Conventions until relatively recently. During this period, State practice began to apply certain general principles of humanitarian law beyond the traditional field of State-to-State conflict to "those internal conflicts that constituted large-scale civil wars."[16] In addition to the Spanish Civil War, events in 1947 during the Civil War between the Communists and the Nationalist régime in China illustrated this new tendency.[17] Common Article 3, which was prepared during this second phase, was apparently addressed to armed conflicts akin to the Chinese and Spanish civil wars. As one commentator has described it, Article 3 was designed to restrain governments "in the handling of armed violence directed against them for the express purpose of secession or at securing a change in the government of a State," but even after the adoption of the Conventions it remained "uncertain whether [Article 3] applied to full-scale civil war."[18]

[15] *Id.* at 505; *see also* Gerald Irving Draper, *Reflections on Law and Armed Conflicts* 107 (1998) ("Before 1949, in the absence of recognized belligerency accorded to the elements opposed to the government of a State, the law of war . . . had no application to internal armed conflicts. . . . International law had little or nothing to say as to how the armed rebellion was crushed by the government concerned, for such matters fell within the domestic jurisdiction of States. Such conflicts were often waged with great lack of restraint and cruelty. Such conduct was a domestic matter.")

[16] *Tadic*, 105 I.I.R. at 507. Indeed, the events of the Spanish Civil War, in which "both the republican Government [of Spain] and third States refused to recognize the [Nationalist] insurgents as belligerents," *id.* at 507, may be reflected in common Article 3's reference to "the legal status of the Parties to the conflict."

[17] *See id.* at 508.

[18] *See* Draper, *Reflections on Law and Armed Conflicts, supra*, at 108.

The third phase represents a more complete break than the second with the traditional "State-sovereignty-oriented approach" of international law. This approach gives central place to individual human rights. As a consequence, it blurs the distinction between international and internal armed conflicts, and even that between civil wars and other forms of internal armed conflict. This approach is well illustrated by the ICTY's decision in *Tadic*, which appears to take the view that common Article 3 applies to non-international armed conflicts of *any* description, and is not limited to civil wars between a State and an insurgent group. In this conception, common Article 3 is not just a complement to common Article 2: rather, it is a catch-all that establishes standards for any and all armed conflicts not included in common Article 2.[19]

[19] An interpretation of common Article 3 that would apply it to all forms of non-international armed conflict accords better with some recent approaches to international humanitarian law. For example, the *Commentary on the Additional Protocols of 8 June 1977 to the Geneva Conventions of 12 August 1949, supra*, after first stating in the text that Article 3 applies when "the government of a single State [is] in conflict with one or more armed factions within its territory," thereafter suggests, in a footnote, that an armed conflict not of an international character "may also exist in which armed factions fight against each other without intervention by the armed forces of the established government." *Id.* ¶ 4339 at n.2. A still broader interpretation appears to be supported by the language of the decision of the International Court of Justice (the "ICJ") in *Nicaragua v. United States*—which, it should be made clear, the United States refused to acknowledge by withdrawing from the compulsory jurisdiction of the ICJ:

> Article 3 which is common to all four Geneva Conventions of 12 August 1949 defines certain rules to be applied *in the armed conflicts of a non-international character*. There is no doubt that, in the event of international armed conflicts, these rules also constitute a minimum yardstick, in addition to the more elaborate rules which are also to apply to international conflicts; and they are rules which,

Nonetheless, despite this recent trend, we think that such an interpretation of common Article 3 fails to take into account, not only the language of the provision, but also its historical context. First, as we have described above, such a reading is inconsistent with the text of Article 3 itself, which applies only to "armed conflict not of an international character occurring in the territory of one of the High Contacting Parties." In conjunction with common Article 2, the text of Article 3 simply does not reach international conflicts where one of the parties is not a Nation State. If we were to read the Geneva Conventions as applying to all forms of armed conflict, we would expect the High Contracting Parties to have used broader language, which they easily could have done. To interpret common Article 3 by expanding its scope well beyond the meaning

---

in the Court's opinion, reflect what the Court in 1949 called "elementary considerations of humanity."

Military and Paramilitary Activities In and Against Nicaragua (Nicaragua v. United States), (International Court of Justice 1986), 76 L.L.R. 1, 448, ¶ 218 (E. Lauterpacht and C.J. Greenwood eds., 1988) (emphasis added). The ICJ's language is probably best read to suggest that all "armed conflicts" are either international or non-international, and that if they are non-international, they are governed by common Article 3. If that is the correct understanding of the quoted language, however, it should be noted that the result was merely stated as a conclusion, without taking account either of the precise language of Article 3 or of the background to its adoption. Moreover, while it was true that one of the conflicts to which the ICJ was addressing itself—"[t]he conflict between the *contras'* forces and those of the Government of Nicaragua"—"was an armed conflict which is 'not of an international character,'" *id.* at 448. ¶ 219, that conflict was recognizably a civil war between a State and an insurgent group, not a conflict between or among violent factions in a territory in which the State had collapsed. Thus there is substantial reason to question the logic and scope of the ICJ's interpretation of common Article 3.

borne by the text is effectively to amend the Geneva Conventions without the approval of the State Parties to the agreements.

Second, as we have discussed, Article 3 was prepared during a period in which the traditional, State-centered view of international law was still dominant and was only just beginning to give way to a human-rights-based approach. Giving due weight to the State practice and doctrinal understanding of the time, it seems to us overwhelmingly likely that an armed conflict between a Nation State and a transnational terrorist organization, or between a Nation State and a failed State harboring and supporting a transnational terrorist organization, could not have been within the contemplation of the drafters of common Article 3. These would have been simply unforeseen and, therefore, not provided for. Indeed, it seems to have been uncertain even a decade after the Conventions were signed whether common Article 3 applied to armed conflicts that were neither international in character nor civil wars but anti-colonialist wars of independence such as those in Algeria and Kenya. *See* Gerald Irving Draper, *The Red Cross Conventions* 15 (1957). Further, it is telling that in order to address this unforeseen circumstance, the State Parties to the Geneva Conventions did not attempt to distort the terms of common Article 3 to apply it to cases that did not fit within its terms. Instead, they drafted two new protocols (neither of which the United States has ratified) to adapt the Conventions to the conditions of contemporary hostilities.[20] Accordingly, common Article 3 is best understood not to apply to such armed conflicts.

[20] See, e.g., Protocol Additional to the Geneva Conventions of 12 August 1949, and Relating to the Protection of Victims of International Armed Conflicts (Protocol I), June 8, 1977, 1125 U.N.T.S. 4: Protocol Additional to the Geneva Conventions of 12 August 1949, and Relating to the Protection of Victims of Non-International Armed Conflicts (Protocol II), June 8, 1977, 1125 U.N.T.S. 610.

January 22, 2002, Jay Bybee

Jay Bybee, assistant attorney general and John Yoo's boss, in a memo prepared for White House Counsel Alberto Gonzales, and William Haynes, General Counsel to the Department of Defense, concludes that the President can decide that Geneva Conventions do not apply in Afghanistan, and that the Taliban and al Qaeda thus fall outside its protections. He argues that the president has the constitutional power to suspend Geneva obligations, that Afghanistan is a failed state and as such the treaty does not apply, and that al Qaeda fighters are not protected because al Qaeda is a non-state actor that cannot enter into treaties. The memo also states that United States forces can modify their Geneva III obligations in light of military necessity. This memo is key to the claim by Rumsfeld and others that they relied on legal advice when they decided to ignore Geneva and permit torture and inhuman treatment as military necessity required.

U.S. Department of Justice
Office of Legal Counsel

Office of the Assistant Attorney General   *Washington, D.C. 20530*

January 22, 2002

Memorandum for Alberto R. Gonzales
Counsel to the President,
and William J. Haynes II
General Counsel of the Department of Defense

RE: *Application of Treaties and Laws to al Qaeda and Taliban Detainees*

You have asked for our Office's views concerning the effect of international treaties and federal laws on the treatment of individuals detained by the U.S. Armed Forces during the conflict in Afghanistan. In particular, you have asked whether certain treaties forming part of the laws of armed conflict apply to the conditions of detention and the procedures for trial of members of al Qaeda and the Taliban militia. We conclude that these treaties do not protect members of the al Qaeda organization, which as a non-State actor cannot be a party to the international agreements governing war. We further conclude that the President has sufficient grounds to find that these treaties do not protect members of the Taliban militia. This memorandum expresses no view as to whether the President should decide, as a matter of policy, that the U.S. Armed Forces should adhere to the standards of conduct in those treaties with respect to the treatment of prisoners.

* * *

IV. Detention Conditions Under Geneva III
Even if the President decided not to suspend our Geneva III obligations toward Afghanistan, two reasons would justify some deviations from the requirements of Geneva III. This would be the case even if Taliban members legally were entitled to POW status. First, *certain deviations concerning treatment can be justified on basic grounds of legal excuse concerning self-defense and feasibility.* Second, the President could choose to find that none of the Taliban prisoners qualify as POWs under Article 4 of Geneva III, which generally defines the types of armed forces that may be considered POWs once captured. In the latter instance, Geneva III would apply and the Afghanistan conflict would fall within common Article 2's jurisdiction. The President, however, would be interpreting the treaty in light of the facts on the ground to find that the Taliban militia categorically failed the test for POWs within Geneva III's terms. We should be clear that we have no information that the conditions of treatment for Taliban *prisoners currently violate Geneva III standards, but it is possible that some*

may argue that our GTMO facilities do not fully comply with all of the treaty's provisions.

A. Justified Deviations from Geneva Convention Requirements

We should make clear that as we understand the facts, the detainees currently are being treated in a manner consistent with common Article 3 of Geneva III. This means that they are housed in basic humane conditions, are not being physically mistreated, and are receiving adequate medical care. They have not yet been tried or punished by any U.S. court system. As a result, the current detention conditions in GTMO do not violate common Article 3, nor do they present a grave breach of Geneva III as defined in Article 130. For purposes of domestic law, therefore, the GTMO conditions do not constitute a violation of the WCA, which criminalizes only violations of common Article 3 or grave breaches of the Conventions.

That said, some may very well argue that detention conditions currently depart from Geneva III requirements. Nonetheless, not all of these deviations from Geneva III would amount to an outright violation of the treaty's requirements. Instead, some departures from the text can be justified by some basic doctrines of legal excuse. *We believe that some deviations would not amount to a treaty violation, because they would be justified by the need for force protection.* Nations have the right to take reasonable steps for the protection of the armed forces guarding prisoners. *At the national level, no treaty can override a nation's inherent right to self-defense.* Indeed, the United Nations Charter recognizes this fundamental principle. Article 51 of the U.N. Charter provides that "[n]othing in the present Charter shall impair the inherent right of individual or collective self-defense if an armed attack occurs against a Member of the United Nations." As we have discussed in other opinions relating to the war on terrorism, the September 11 attacks on the

Pentagon and the World Trade Center have triggered the United States' right to defend itself.[1] Our national right to self-defense must encompass the lesser included right to defend our own forces from prisoners who pose a threat to their lives and safety, just as the Nation has the authority to take measures in the field to protect the U.S. armed forces. Any Geneva III obligations, therefore, may be legally adjusted to take into account the needs of force protection.

The right to national self-defense is further augmented by the individual right to self-defense as a justification for modifications to Geneva III based on the need for force protection. Under domestic law, self-defense serves *as a legal defense even to the taking of a human life.* "[S]elf defense is . . . embodied in our jurisprudence as a consideration totally eliminating any criminal taint. . . . It is difficult to the point of impossibility to imagine a right in any state to abolish self defense altogether. . . ."[2] As the U.S. Court of Appeals for the District of Columbia Circuit has observed, "[m]ore than two centuries ago, Blackstone, best known of the expositors of the English common law, taught that 'all homicide is malicious, and of course, amounts to murder, unless . . . *excused* on the

[1] Memorandum for Alberto R. Gonzales, Counsel to the President, from Patrick F. Philbin, Deputy Attorney General, Office of Legal Counsel, *Re: Legality of the Use of Military Commissions to Try Terrorists* at 22–33 (Nov. 6, 2001); Memorandum for Alberto R. Gonzales, Counsel to the President and William J. Haynes, II, General Counsel, Department of Defense, from John C. Yoo, Deputy Assistant Attorney General and Robert J. Delahunty, Special Counsel, Office of Legal Counsel, *Re: Authority for Use of Military Force to Combat Terrorist Activities Within the United States* at 2–3 (Oct. 17, 2001).

[2] *Griffin v. Mortin,* 785 F.2d 1172, 1186–87 & n.37 (4th Cir. 1986), *aff'd by an equality divided court,* 795 F.2d 22 (4th Cir. 1986) (en banc), *cert. denied,* 480 U.S. 919 (1987).

account of accident or self-preservation. . . .' Self-defense, as a doctrine legally exonerating the taking of human life, is as viable now as it was in Blackstone's time. . . ."[3] Both the Supreme Court and this Office have opined that the use of force by law enforcement or the military is constitutional, even if it results in the loss of life, if necessary to protect the lives and safety of officers or innocent third parties.[4] Thus, as a matter of domestic law, the United States armed forces can modify their Geneva III obligations to take into account the needs of military necessity to protect their individual members.

Other deviations from Geneva III, which do not involve force protection, may still be justified as a domestic legal matter on the ground that immediate compliance is infeasible. Certain conditions, we have been informed, are only temporary until the Defense Department can construct permanent facilities that will be in compliance with Geneva. We believe that no treaty breach would exist under such circumstances. The State Department has informed us that state practice under the Convention allows nations a period of reasonable time to satisfy their affirmative obligations for treatment

[3] *United States v. Peterson,* 483 F.2d 1222, 1228–29 (D.C. Cir.) (footnote omitted), *cert denied,* 414 U.S. 1007 (1973).

[4] *See Tennessee v. Garner,* 471 U.S. 1, 7, 11 (1985) (Fourth Amendment "seizure" caused by use of force subject to reasonableness analysis); Memorandum to Files, from Robert Delahunty, Special Counsel, Office of Legal Counsel, *Re: Use of Deadly Force Against Civil Aircraft Threatening to Attack 1996 Summer Olympic Games* (Aug. 19, 1996); *United States Assistance to Countries that Shoot Down Civil Aircraft Involved in Drug Trafficking,* 18 Op. O.L.C. 148, 164 (1994) ("[A] USG officer or employee may use deadly force against civil aircraft without violating [a criminal statute] if he or she reasonably believes that the aircraft poses a threat of serious physical harm . . . to another person.").

of POWs, particularly during the early stages of a conflict.[5] An analogy can be drawn here to a similar legal doctrine in administrative law. For example, it is a well-established principle that, where a statutory mandate fails to specify a particular deadline for agency action, a federal agency's duty to comply with that mandate is lawfully discharged, as long as it is satisfied within a reasonable time. The Administrative Procedure Act expressly provides that a "reviewing court shall . . . compel agency action unlawfully withheld or *unreasonably* delayed." 5 U.S.C. § 706 (emphasis added). Courts have recognized accordingly that a federal agency has a reasonable time to discharge its obligations.[6] Thus, "if an agency has no concrete deadline establishing a date by which it must act, . . . a court must compel only action that is delayed unreasonably. . . . [W]hen an agency is required to act—either by organic statute or by the APA—within an expeditious, prompt, or reasonable time, § 706 leaves in the courts the discretion to decide whether agency delay is unreasonable."[7]

*   *   *

[5] During the India-Pakistan conflicts between 1965 and 1971, prisoners were able to correspond with their families, but there were "some difficulties in getting lists of all military prisoners"—"[e]specially at the beginning of the conflict," Allan Rosas, *The Legal Status of Prisoners of War* at 186 (1976). Similarly, during the 1967 War in the Middle East, Israeli authorities delayed access to Arab prisoners on the grounds that "all facilities would be granted as soon as the prisoners were transferred to the camp at Atlith . . . In the meantime, delegates had the opportunity to see some of the prisoners at the transit camp at El Quantara and Kusseima." *Id.* at 203 (citation omitted). Although Israel was technically obliged under the Convention to provide access to Arab. POWs, immediate compliance with that obligation was infeasible.

[6] *Sierra Club v. Thomas,* 828 F.2d 783, 794 (D. C. Cir. 1987).

[7] *Forest Guardians v. Babbitt,* 174 F.3d 1178, 1190 (10th Cir 1999).

Conclusion

For the foregoing reasons, we conclude that neither the federal War Crimes Act nor the Geneva Conventions would apply to the detention conditions of al Qaeda prisoners. We also conclude that the President has the plenary constitutional power to suspend our treaty obligations toward Afghanistan during the period of the conflict. He may exercise that discretion on the basis that Afghanistan was a failed State. Even if he chose not to, he could interpret Geneva III to find that members of the Taliban militia failed to qualify as POWs under the terms of the treaty. We also conclude that customary international law has no binding legal effect on either the President or the military because it is not federal law, as recognized by the Constitution.

We should make clear that in reaching a decision to suspend our treaty obligations or to construe Geneva III to conclude that members of the Taliban militia are not POWs, the President need not make any specific finding. Rather, he need only authorize or approve policies that would be consistent with the understanding that al Qaeda and Taliban prisoners are not POWs under Geneva III.

Please let us know if we can provide further assistance.

Jay S. Bybee
Assistant Attorney General

January 25, 2002, Alberto Gonzales

In this memo to George Bush, Alberto Gonzales, White House counsel, confirms and endorses the Yoo and Bybee opinion that the Geneva Conventions do not apply to either al Qaeda or the Taliban, and discounts Secretary of State Colin Powell's dissenting memo. Therefore, they are not to be recognized as prisoners of war—which is an internationally and legally recognized term meaning they are kept in communal camps, cannot be prosecuted except for violations of the laws of war, and receive humane treatment. President Bush later labeled them "unlawful combatants," which, in practice, means the administration can do what it wants to them.

Gonzales, as senior to both Yoo and Bybee, could have overridden their memoranda but instead chose to affirm their legal arguments. This is the memo in which Gonzales characterizes sections of the Geneva Conventions as "obsolete" and "quaint" and states that the Geneva Conventions can be departed from if military necessity so requires. This is also the memo in which Gonzales argues that it might be important to find Geneva not applicable to avoid the possibility of having officials in the military and others accused of war crimes for violation of Geneva.

DRAFT
1/25/2002–3:30 pm

January 25, 2002

MEMORANDUM FOR THE PRESIDENT

FROM: ALBERTO R. GONZALES

SUBJECT: DECISION RE APPLICATION OF THE GENEVA
              CONVENTION ON PRISONERS OF WAR TO THE
              CONFLICT WITH AL QAEDA AND THE TALIBAN

Purpose

On January 18, I advised you that the Department of Justice had issued a formal legal opinion concluding that the Geneva Convention III on the Treatment of Prisoners of War (GPW) does not apply to the conflict with al Qaeda. I also advised you that DOJ's opinion concludes that there are reasonable grounds for you to conclude that GPW does not apply with respect to the conflict with the Taliban. I understand that you decided that GPW does not apply and, accordingly, that al Qaeda and Taliban detainees are not prisoners of war under the GPW.

The Secretary of State has requested that you reconsider that decision. Specifically, he has asked that you conclude that GPW does apply to both al Qaeda and the Taliban. I understand, however, that he would agree that al Qaeda and Taliban fighters could be determined not to be prisoners of war (POWs) but only on a case-by-case basis following individual hearings before a military board.

This memorandum outlines the ramifications of your decision and the Secretary's request for reconsideration.

Legal Background

As an initial matter, I note that you have the constitutional authority to make the determination you made on January 18 that the GPW does not apply to al Qaeda and the Taliban. (Of course, you could nevertheless, as a matter of policy, decide to apply the principles of GPW to the conflict with al Qaeda and the Taliban.) The Office of Legal Counsel of the Department of Justice has opined that, as a matter of international and domestic law, GPW does not apply to the conflict with al Qaeda. OLC has further opined that you have the authority to determine that GPW does not apply to the Taliban. As I discussed with you, the grounds for such a determination may include:

- A determination that Afghanistan was a failed State because the Taliban did not exercise full control over the territory and people, was not recognized by the international community, and was not capable of fulfilling its international obligations (e.g., was in widespread material breach of its international obligations).

- A determination that the Taliban and its forces were, in fact, not a government, but a militant, terrorist-like group.

OLC's interpretation of this legal issue is definitive. The Attorney General is charged by statute with interpreting the law for the Executive Branch. This interpretive authority extends to both domestic and international law. He has, in turn, delegated this role to OLC. Nevertheless, you should be aware that the Legal Adviser to the Secretary of State has expressed a different view.

Ramifications of Determination that GPW Does Not Apply

The consequences of a decision to adhere to what I understood to be your earlier determination that the GPW does not apply to the Taliban include the following:

Positive:

- Preserves flexibility:
  - As you have said, the war against terrorism is a new kind of war. It is not the traditional clash between nations adhering to the laws of war that formed the backdrop for GPW. The nature of the new war places a high premium on other factors, such as the ability to quickly obtain information from captured terrorists and their sponsors in order to avoid further atrocities against American civilians, and the need to try terrorists for war crimes such as wantonly killing civilians. *In my judgment, this new paradigm renders obsolete Geneva's strict limitations on questioning of enemy prisoners and renders quaint some of its* provisions requiring that captured

enemy be afforded such things as commissary privileges, scrip (i.e., advances of monthly pay), athletic uniforms, and scientific instruments.

- Although some of these provisions do not apply to detainees who are not POWs, a determination that GPW does not apply to al Qaeda and the Taliban eliminates any argument regarding the need for case-by-case determinations of POW status. It also holds open options for the future conflicts in which it may be more difficult to determine whether an enemy force as a whole meets the standard for POW status.
- By concluding that GPW does not apply to al Qaeda and the Taliban, we avoid foreclosing options for the future, particularly against nonstate actors.

■ Substantially reduces the threat of domestic criminal prosecution under the War Crimes Act (18 U.S.C. 2441).

- That statute, enacted in 1996, prohibits the commission of a "war crime" by or against a U.S. person, including U.S. officials. "War crime" for these purposes is defined to include any grave breach of GPW or any violation of common Article 3 thereof (such as "outrages against personal dignity"). Some of these provisions apply (if the GPW applies) regardless of whether the individual being detained qualifies as a POW. Punishments for violations of Section 2441 include the death penalty. A determination that the GPW is not applicable to the Taliban would mean that Section 2441 would not apply to actions taken with respect to the Taliban.
- Adhering to your determination that GPW does not apply would guard effectively against misconstruction or misapplication of Section 2441 for several reasons.
- First, some of the language of the GPW is undefined (it prohibits, for example, "outrages upon personal

dignity" and "inhuman treatment"), and it is difficult to predict with confidence what actions might be deemed to constitute violations of the relevant provisions of GPW.

- Second, it is difficult to predict the needs and circumstances that could arise in the course of the war on terrorism.

- Third, it is difficult to predict the motives of prosecutors and independent counsels who may in the future decide to pursue unwarranted charges based on Section 2441. Your determination would create a reasonable basis in law that Section 2441 does not apply, which would provide a solid defense to any future prosecution.

Negative:

On the other hand, the following arguments would support reconsideration and reversal of your decision that the GPW does not apply to either al Qaeda or the Taliban:

- Since the Geneva Conventions were concluded in 1949, the United States has never denied their applicability to either U.S. or opposing forces engaged in armed conflict, despite several opportunities to do so. During the last Bush Administration, the United States stated that it "has a policy of applying the Geneva Conventions of 1949 whenever armed hostilities occur with regular foreign armed forces, even if arguments could be made that the threshold standards for the applicability of the Conventions . . . are not met."

- The United States could not invoke the GPW if enemy forces threatened to mistreat or mistreated U.S. or coalition forces captured during operations in Afghanistan, or if they denied Red Cross access or other POW privileges.

- The War Crimes Act could not be used against the enemy, although other criminal statutes and the customary law of war would still be available.
- Our position would likely provoke widespread condemnation among our allies and in some domestic quarters, even if we make clear that we will comply with the core humanitarian principles of the treaty as a matter of policy.
- Concluding that the Geneva Convention does not apply may encourage other countries to look for technical "loopholes" in future conflicts to conclude that they are not bound by GPW either
- Other countries may be less inclined to turn over terrorists or provide legal assistance to us if we do not recognize a legal obligation to comply with the GPW.
- A determination that GPW does not apply to al Qaeda and the Taliban could undermine U.S. military culture which emphasizes maintaining the highest standards of conduct in combat, and could introduce an element of uncertainty in the status of adversaries.

Response to arguments for Applying GPW to the al Qaeda and the Taliban

On balance, I believe that the arguments for reconsideration and reversal are unpersuasive.

- The argument that the U.S. has never determined that GPW did not apply is incorrect. In at least one case (Panama in 1989) the U.S. determined that GPW did not apply even though it determined for policy reasons to adhere to the convention. More importantly, as noted above, this is a new type of warfare—one not contemplated in 1949 when the GPW was framed—and requires a new approach in our actions toward captured terrorists. Indeed, as the statement quoted from the administration of President George Bush makes clear, the U.S. will apply GPW "whenever hostilities occur *with regular foreign armed forces.*" By its terms, therefore; the policy does not apply to a conflict with terrorists, or with irregular forces, like the Taliban, who are armed militants that oppressed and terrorized the people of Afghanistan.

- In response to the argument that we should decide to apply GPW to the Taliban in order to encourage other countries to treat captured U.S. military personnel in accordance with the GPW, it should be noted that your policy of providing humane treatment to enemy detainees gives us the credibility to insist on like treatment for our soldiers. Moreover, even if GPW is not applicable, we can still bring war crimes charges against anyone who mistreats U.S. personnel. Finally, I note that our adversaries in several recent conflicts have not been deterred by GPW in their mistreatment of captured U.S. personnel, and terrorists will not follow GPW rules in any event.

- The statement that other nations would criticize the U.S. because we have determined that GPW does not apply is undoubtedly true. It is even possible that some nations would point to that determination as a basis for failing to cooperate with us on specific matters in the war against terrorism. On the other hand, some international and domestic criticism is already likely to flow from your previous decision not to treat the detainees as POWs. And we can facilitate cooperation with other nations by reassuring them that we fully support GPW where it is applicable and by acknowledging that in this conflict the U.S. continues to respect other recognized standards.

- In the treatment of detainees, the U.S. will continue to be constrained by (i) its commitment to treat the detainees *humanely and, to the extent appropriate and consistent with military necessity, in a manner consistent with the principles of GPW,* (ii) its applicable treaty obligations, (iii) minimum standards of treatment universally recognized by the nations of the world, and (iv) applicable military regulations regarding the treatment of detainees.
- Similarly, the argument based on military culture fails to recognize that our military remain bound to apply the principles of GPW because that is what you have directed them to do.

February 7, 2002, George W. Bush

This short memo details the president's finding, two weeks after receiving the analysis of his counsel, Alberto Gonzales, that the Geneva Conventions do not apply to Al Qaeda. In this memo, Bush endorses the view that the Taliban detainees are "unlawful combatants,"—which is not a legal category but a term coined by the administration. As such, the president states, the Taliban do not qualify as prisoners of war.

The memo also states that detainees are to be treated humanely to "the extent appropriate and consistent with military necessity." This is what defendants argue justifies their inhumane treatment of detainees.

The White House

Washington

February 7, 2002

MEMORANDUM FOR THE VICE PRESIDENT

    THE SECRETARY OF STATE

    THE SECRETARY OF DEFENSE

    THE ATTORNEY GENERAL

    CHIEF OF STAFF TO THE PRESIDENT

    DIRECTOR OF CENTRAL INTELLIGENCE

    ASSISTANT TO THE PRESIDENT FOR NATIONAL SECURITY AFFAIRS

    CHAIRMAN OF THE JOINT CHIEFS OF STAFF

SUBJECT: Humane Treatment of al Qaeda and Taliban Detainees

1. Our recent extensive discussions regarding the status of al Qaeda and Taliban detainees confirm that the application of the Geneva Convention Relative to the Treatment of Prisoners of War of August 12, 1949 (Geneva) to the conflict with al Qaeda and the Taliban involves complex legal questions. By its terms, Geneva applies to conflicts involving "High

Contracting Parties," which can only be States. Moreover, it assumes the existence of "regular" armed forces fighting on behalf of States. However, the war against terrorism ushers in a new paradigm, one in which groups with broad, international reach commit horrific acts against innocent civilians, sometimes with the direct support of States. Our Nation recognizes that this new paradigm—ushered in not by us, but by terrorists—requires new thinking in the law of war, but thinking that should nevertheless be consistent with the principles of Geneva.

2. Pursuant to my authority as Commander-in-Chief and Chief Executive of the United States, and relying on the opinion of the Department of Justice dated January 22, 2002, and on the legal opinion rendered by the Attorney General in his letter of February 1, 2002, I hereby determine as follows:

   a. I accept the legal conclusion of the Department of Justice and determine that none of the provisions of Geneva apply to our conflict with al Qaeda in Afghanistan or elsewhere throughout the world because, among other reasons, al Qaeda is not a High Contracting Party to Geneva.

   b. I accept the legal conclusion of the Attorney General and the Department of Justice that I have the authority under the Constitution to suspend Geneva as between the United States and Afghanistan, but I decline to exercise that authority at this time. Accordingly, I determine that the provisions of Geneva will apply to our present conflict with the Taliban. I reserve the right to exercise this authority in this or future conflicts.

   c. I also accept the legal conclusion of the Department of Justice and determine that common Article 3 of Geneva does not apply to either al Qaeda or Taliban detainees, because, among other reasons, the relevant conflicts are international in scope and common Article 3 applies only to "armed conflict not of an international character."

    d. Based on the facts supplied by the Department of Defense and the recommendation of the Department of Justice, I determine that the Taliban detainees are unlawful combatants and, therefore, do not qualify as prisoners of war under Article 4 of Geneva. I note that, because Geneva does not apply to our conflict with al Qaeda, al Qaeda detainees also do not qualify as prisoners of war.

3. Of course, our values as a Nation, values that we share with many nations in the world, call *for us to treat detainees humanely, including* those who are not *legally entitled to such treatment.* Our Nation has been and will continue to be a strong supporter of Geneva and its principles. As a matter of policy, the United States Armed Forces shall *continue to treat detainees humanely and, to the extent appropriate and consistent with military necessity, in a manner consistent with the principles of Geneva.*

4. The United States will hold states, organizations, and individuals who gain control of United States personnel responsible for treating such personnel humanely and consistent with applicable law.

5. I hereby reaffirm the order previously issued by the Secretary of Defense to the United States Armed Forces requiring that the detainees be treated humanely and, to the extent appropriate and consistent with military necessity, in a manner consistent with the principles of Geneva.

6. I hereby direct the Secretary of State to communicate my determinations in an appropriate manner to our allies, and other countries and international organizations cooperating in the war against terrorism of global reach.

[Signed George Bush]

August 1, 2002, Jay Bybee and John Yoo,
aka the "Torture Memo"

In this excerpt from a lengthy memo, to Counsel to the President Alberto Gonzales, written several months after the first set of memos excerpted earlier, co-authors Assistant Attorney General Jay Bybee and Deputy Assistant Attorney General John Yoo, set forth their views regarding the president's authority to order harsh interrogation methods and redefine what is meant by torture. Initially, the administration memos were written to overcome the War Crimes Statute, which criminalizes torture.

This memo, however, was written to address Vice President Cheney's concerns that the CIA was unwilling to interrogate alleged al Qaeda suspects, such as Abu Zubayadh, in a sufficiently harsh manner, and to overcome the CIA's opposition to techniques that it believed violated the Convention Against Torture.

The memo concludes that necessity or self-defense may justify interrogation methods that would otherwise be a crime under the Torture Statute. It also concludes that to constitute torture under the Torture Statute, the methods must generate pain "of an intensity to that which accompanies physical injury such as death or organ failure." As far as mental pain, torture requires not just pain at the moment it is inflicted, but "lasting psychological harm such as seen in post-traumatic stress disorder." This memo was written to the president's counsel Alberto Gonzales and it is the defendants' belief that their reliance on this memo exonerates them from the commission of the crime of torture.

U.S Department of Justice
Office of Legal Counsel

Office of the Assistant Attorney General   *Washington, D.C. 20530*

August 1, 2002

Memorandum for Alberto R. Gonzales Counsel
to the President

RE: *Standards of Conduct for Interrogation under 18 U.S.C.*
        §§2340–2340A

You have asked for our Office's views regarding the standards of conduct under the Convention Against Torture and Other Cruel, Inhuman and Degrading Treatment or Punishment as implemented by Sections 2340–2340A of title 18 of the United States Code. As we understand it, this question has arisen in the context of the conduct of interrogations outside of the United States. We conclude below that Section 2340A proscribes acts inflicting, and that are specifically intended to inflict, severe pain or suffering, whether mental or physical. Those acts must be of an extreme nature to rise to the level of torture within the meaning of Section 2340A and the Convention. We further conclude that certain acts may be cruel, inhuman, or degrading, but still not produce pain and suffering of the requisite intensity to fall within Section 2340A's proscription against torture. We conclude by examining possible defenses that would negate any claim that certain interrogation methods violate the statute.

In Part I, we examine the criminal stature's text and history. We conclude that for an act to constitute torture as defined in Section 2340, it must inflict pain that is difficult to endure. Physical pain amounting to torture must be equivalent in intensity to the pain accompanying serious physical injury, such as organ failure, impairment of bodily function, or even death. For purely mental pain or suffering to amount to torture under Section 2340, it must result in significant psychological harm of significant duration, e.g., lasting for months or even years. We conclude that the mental harm also must result from one of the predicate acts listed in the statute, namely: threats of imminent death; threats of infliction of the kind of pain that would amount to physical torture; infliction of such physical pain as a means of psychological torture; use of drugs or other procedures designed to deeply disrupt the senses, or fundamentally alter an individual's personality; or threatening to do any of these things to a third party. The legislative history simply reveals that Congress intended for the statute's definition to track the Convention's definition of torture and the reservations, understandings, and declarations that the United States submitted with its ratification. We conclude that the statute, taken as a whole, makes plain that it prohibits only extreme acts.

In Part II, we examine the text, ratification history, and negotiating history of the Torture Convention. We conclude that the treaty's text prohibits only the most extreme acts by reserving criminal penalties solely for torture and declining to require such penalties for "cruel, inhuman, or degrading treatment or punishment." This confirms our view that the criminal statute penalizes only the most egregious conduct. Executive branch interpretations and representations to the Senate at the time of ratification further confirm that the treaty was intended to reach only the most extreme conduct.

In Part III, we analyze the jurisprudence of the Torture Victims Protection Act, 28 U.S.C. § 1350 note (2000), which provides civil remedies for torture victims, to predict the standards that courts might follow in determining what actions reach the threshold of torture in the criminal context. We conclude from these cases that courts are likely to take a totality-of-the-circumstances approach, and will look to an entire course of conduct, to determine whether certain acts will violate Section 2340A. Moreover, these cases demonstrate that most often torture involves cruel and extreme physical pain. In Part IV, we examine international decisions regarding the use of sensory deprivation techniques. These cases make clear that while many of these techniques may amount to cruel, inhuman or degrading treatment, they do not produce pain or suffering of the necessary intensity to meet the definition of torture. From these decisions, we conclude that there is a wide range of such techniques that will not rise to the level of torture.

In Part V, we discuss whether Section 2340A may be unconstitutional if applied to interrogations undertaken of enemy combatants pursuant to the President's Commander-in-Chief powers. We find that in the circumstances of the current war against al Qaeda and its allies, prosecution under Section 2340A may be barred because enforcement of the statute would represent an unconstitutional infringement of the President's authority to conduct war. In Part VI, we discuss defenses to an allegation that an interrogation method might violate the statute. We conclude that, under the current circumstances, necessity or self-defense may justify interrogation methods that might violate Section 2340A.

I. 18 U.S.C. §§2340–2340A

Section 2340A makes it a criminal offense for any person "outside the United States [to] commit or attempt to commit torture."[1] Section 2340 defines the act of torture as an:

[1]If convicted of torture, a defendant faces a fine or up to twenty years' imprisonment or both. If, however, the act resulted in the victim's death, a defendant may be sentenced to life imprisonment or to death. *See* 18 U.S.C.A. §2340A(a). Whether death results from the act also affects the applicable statute of limitations. Where death does not result, the statute of

act committed by a person acting under the color of law specifically intended to inflict severe physical or mental pain or suffering (other than pain or suffering incidental to lawful sanctions) upon another person within his custody or physical control.

*   *   *

VI. Defenses

In the foregoing parts of this memorandum, we have demonstrated that the ban on torture in Section 2340A is limited to only the most extreme forms of physical and mental harm. We have also demonstrated that Section 2340A, as applied to interrogations of enemy combatants ordered by the President pursuant to his Commander-in-Chief power would be unconstitutional. Even if an interrogation method, however, might arguably cross the line drawn in Section 2340, and application of the statute was not held to be an unconstitutional infringement of the President's Commander-in-Chief authority, we believe that under the current

---

limitations is eight years; if death results, there is no statute of limitations. See 18 U.S.C.A. §3286(b) (West Supp. 2002); id. §2332b(g)(5)(B) (West Supp. 2002). Section 2340A as originally enacted did not provide for the death penalty as a punishment. See Omnibus Crime Bill, Pub. L. No. 103–322, Title VI, Section 60020, 108 Stat. 1979 (1994) (amending section 2340A to provide for the death penalty); H. R. Conf. Rep. No. 103–711, at 388 (1994) (noting that the act added the death penalty as a penalty for torture).

Most recently, the USA Patriot Act, Pub. L. No. 107–56, 115 Stat. 272 (2001), amended section 2340A to expressly codify the offense of conspiracy to commit torture. Congress enacted this amendment as part of a broader effort to ensure that individuals engaged in the planning of terrorist activities could be prosecuted irrespective of where the activities took place. See H. R. Rep. No. 107–236, at 70 (2001) (discussing the addition of "conspiracy" as a separate offense for a variety of "Federal terrorism offense[s]").

circumstances certain justification defenses might be available that would potentially eliminate criminal liability. Standard criminal law defenses of necessity and self-defense could justify interrogation methods needed to elicit information to prevent a direct and imminent threat to the United States and its citizens.

A. Necessity

We believe that a defense of necessity could be raised, under the current circumstances, to an allegation of a Section 2340A violation. Often referred to as the "choice of evils" defense, necessity has been defined as follows:

> Conduct that the actor believes to be necessary to avoid a harm or evil to himself or to another is justifiable, provided that:
>
> (a) the harm or evil sought to be avoided by such conduct is greater than that sought to be prevented by the law defining the offense charged; and
> (b) neither the Code nor other law defining the offense provides exceptions or defenses dealing with the specific situation involved; and
> (c) a legislative purpose to exclude the justification claimed does not otherwise plainly appear.

Model Penal Code § 3.02. *See also* Wayne R. LaFave & Austin W. Scott, 1 Substantive Criminal Law § 5.4 at 627 (1986 & 2002 supp.) ("LaFave & Scott"). Although there is no federal statute that generally establishes necessity or other justification as defenses to federal criminal laws, the Supreme Court has recognized the defense. *See United States v. Bailey,* 444 U.S. 394, 410 (1980) (relying on LaFave & Scott and Model Penal Code definitions of necessity defense).

The necessity defense may prove especially relevant in the current circumstances. As it has been described in the case law and literature, the purpose behind necessity is one of public policy. According to LaFave and Scott, "[t]he law ought to promote the achievement of higher values at the expense of lesser values, and sometimes the greater good for society will be accomplished by violating the literal language of the criminal law." LaFave & Scott, at 629. In particular, the necessity defense can justify the intentional killing of one person to save two others because "it is better that two lives be saved and one lost than that two be lost and one saved." *Id.* Or, put in the language of a choice of evils, "the evil involved in violating the terms of the criminal law (. . . even taking another's life) may be less than that which would result from literal compliance with the law (. . . two lives lost)." *Id.*

Additional elements of the necessity defense are worth noting here. First, the defense is not limited to certain types of harms. Therefore, the harm inflicted by necessity may include intentional homicide, so long as the harm avoided is greater (i.e., preventing more deaths). *Id.* at 634. Second, it must actually be the defendant's intention to avoid the greater harm; intending to commit murder and then learning only later that the death had the fortuitous result of saving other lives will not support a necessity defense. *Id.* at 635. Third, if the defendant reasonably believed that the lesser harm was necessary, even if, unknown to him, it was not, he may still avail himself of the defense. As LaFave and Scott explain, "if A kills B reasonably believing it to be necessary to save C and D, he is not guilty of murder even though, unknown to A, C and D could have been rescued without the necessity of killing B." *Id.* Fourth, it is for the court, and not the defendant to judge whether the harm avoided outweighed the harm done. *Id.* at 636. Fifth, the defendant cannot rely upon the necessity defense if a third alternative is open and known to him that will cause less harm.

It appears to us that under the current circumstances the necessity defense could be successfully maintained in response to an allegation of a Section 2340A violation. On September 11, 2001, al Qaeda launched a surprise covert attack on civilian targets in the United States that led to the deaths of thousands and losses in billions of dollars. According to public and governmental reports, al Qaeda has other sleeper cells within the United States that may be planning similar attacks. Indeed, al Qaeda plans apparently include efforts to develop and deploy chemical, biological and nuclear weapons of mass destruction. Under these circumstances, a detainee may possess information that could enable the United States to prevent attacks that potentially could equal or surpass the September 11 attacks in their magnitude. Clearly, any harm that might occur during an interrogation would pale to insignificance compared to the harm avoided by preventing such an attack, which could take hundreds or thousands of lives.

Under this calculus, two factors will help indicate when the necessity defense could appropriately be invoked. First, the more certain that government officials are that a particular individual has information needed to prevent an attack, the more necessary interrogation will be. Second, the more likely it appears to be that a terrorist attack is likely to occur, and the greater the amount of damage expected from such an attack, the more that an interrogation to get information would become necessary. Of course, the strength of the necessity defense depends on the circumstances that prevail, and the knowledge of the government actors involved, when the interrogation is conducted. While every interrogation that might violate Section 2340A does not trigger a necessity defense, we can say that certain circumstances could support such a defense.

Legal authorities identify an important exception to the necessity defense. The defense is available "only in situations wherein the legislature has not itself, in its criminal statute, made a determination of values." *Id.* at 629. Thus, if Congress explicitly has made clear that violation of a statute cannot be outweighed by the harm avoided, courts cannot recognize the necessity defense. LaFave and Israel provide as an example an abortion statute that made clear that abortions even to save the life of the mother would still be a crime; in such cases the necessity defense would be unavailable. *Id.* at 630. Here, however, Congress has not explicitly made a determination of values vis-à-vis torture. In fact, Congress explicitly removed efforts to remove torture from the weighing of values permitted by the necessity defense.[2]

---

[2] In the CAT, torture is defined as the intentional infliction of severe pain or suffering "for such purpose as obtaining from him or a third person information or a confession." CAT Article 1.1. One could argue that such a definition represented an attempt to indicate that the good of of obtaining information—no matter what the circumstances—could not justify an act of torture. In other words, necessity would not be a defense. In enacting Section 2340, however, Congress removed the purpose element in the definition of torture, evidencing an intention to remove any fixing of values by statute. By leaving Section 2340 silent as to the harm done by torture in comparison to other harms, Congress allowed the necessity defense to apply when appropriate.

Further, the CAT contains an additional provision that "no exceptional circumstances whatsoever, whether a state of war or a threat of war, internal political instability or any other public emergency, may be invoked as a justification of torture." CAT Article 2.2. Aware of this provision of the treaty, and of the definition of the necessity defense that allows the legislature to provide for an exception to the defense, see Model Penal Code § 3.02(b), Congress did not incorporate CAT Article 2.2 into Section 2340. Given that Congress omitted CAT's effort to bar a necessity or wartime defense, we read Section 2340 as permitting the defense.

B. Self-Defense

Even if a court were to find that a violation of Section 2340A was not justified by necessity, a defendant could still appropriately raise a claim of self-defense. The right to self-defense, even when it involves deadly force, is deeply embedded in our law, both as to individuals and as to the nation as a whole. As the Court of Appeals for the D.C. Circuit has explained:

> More than two centuries ago, Blackstone, best known of the expositors of the English common law, taught that "all homicide is malicious, and of course amounts to murder, unless . . . excused on the account of accident or self-preservation . . ." Self-defense, as a doctrine legally exonerating the taking of human life, is as viable now as it was in Blackstone's time.

United States v. Peterson, 483 F.2d 1222, 1228–29 (D.C. Cir. 1973). Self-defense is a common-law defense to federal criminal law offenses, and nothing in the text, structure or history of Section 2340A precludes its application to a charge of torture. In the absence of any textual provision to the contrary, we assume self-defense can be an appropriate defense to an allegation of torture.

The doctrine of self-defense permits the use of force to prevent harm to another person. As LaFave and Scott explain, "one is justified in using reasonable force in defense of another person, even a stranger, when he reasonably believes that the other is in immediate danger of unlawful bodily harm from his adversary and that the use of such force is necessary to avoid this danger." *Id.* at 663–64. Ultimately, even deadly force is permissible, but "only when the attack of the adversary upon the other person reasonably appears to the defender to be a deadly attack." *Id.* at 664. As with our discussion of necessity, we will review the significant elements of this defense.[3] According to LaFave and Scott, the elements of the defense of others are the same as those that apply to individual self-defense.

First, self-defense requires that the use of force be *necessary* to avoid the danger of unlawful bodily harm. *Id.* at 649. A defender may justifiably use deadly force if he reasonably believes that the other person is about to inflict unlawful death or serious bodily harm upon another, and that it is necessary to use such force to prevent it. *Id.* at 652. Looked at from the opposite perspective, the defender may not use force when the force would be as equally effective at a later time and the defender suffers no harm or risk by waiting. *See* Paul H. Robinson, 2 Criminal Law Defenses § 131(c) at 77 (1984). If, however, other options permit the defender to retreat safely from a confrontation without having to resort to deadly force, the use of force may not be necessary in the first place. La Fave and Scott at 659–60.

Second, self-defense requires that the defendant's belief in the necessity of using force be reasonable. If a defendant honestly but unreasonably believed force was necessary, he will not be able to make out a successful claim of self-defense. *Id.* at 654. Conversely, if a defendant reasonably believed an attack was to occur, but the facts subsequently showed no attack was threatened, he may still raise self-defense. As LaFave and Scott explain," one may be justified in shooting to death an adversary who, having threatened to kill him, reaches for his pocket as if for a gun, though it later appears that he had no gun and that he was only reaching for his handkerchief." *Id.* Some authorities, such as the Model Penal Code, even eliminate the reasonability element, and require only that the

---

[3] Early cases had suggested that in order to be eligible for defense of another, one should have some personal relationship with the one in need of protection. That view has been discarded. LaFave & Scott at 664.

defender honestly believed—regardless of its unreasonableness—that the use of force was necessary.

Third, many legal authorities include the requirement that a defender must reasonably believe that the unlawful violence is "imminent" before he can use force in his defense. It would be a mistake, however, to equate imminence necessarily with timing—that an attack is immediately about to occur. Rather, as the Model Penal Code explains, what is essential is that, the defensive *response* must be "immediately necessary." Model Penal Code § 3.04(1). Indeed, imminence may be merely another way of expressing the requirement of necessity. Robinson at 78. LaFave and Scott, for example, believe that the imminence requirement makes sense as part of a necessity defense because if an attack is not immediately upon the defender, the defender has other options available to avoid the attack that do not involve the use of force. LaFave and Scott at 656. If, however, the fact of the attack becomes certain and no other options remain, the use of force may be justified. To use a well-known hypothetical, if A were to kidnap and confine B, and then tell B he would kill B one week later, B would be justified in using force in self-defense, even if the opportunity arose before the week had passed. *Id.* at 656; *see also* Robinson at § 131(c)(1) at 78. In this hypothetical situation, while the attack itself is not imminent, B's use of force becomes immediately necessary whenever he has an opportunity to save himself from A.

Fourth, the amount of force should be proportional to the threat. As LaFave and Scott explain, "the amount of force which [the defender] may justifiably use must be reasonably related to the threatened harm which he seeks to avoid." LaFave and Scott at 651. Thus, one may not use deadly force in response to a threat that does not rise to death or serious bodily harm. If such harm may result, however, deadly force is appropriate. As the Model Penal Code § 3.04(2)(b) states, "[the] use of deadly force is not justifiable . . . unless the actor believes that such force is necessary to protect himself against death, serious bodily injury, kidnapping or sexual intercourse compelled by force or threat."

Under the current circumstances, we believe that a defendant accused of violating Section 2340A could have, in certain circumstances, grounds to properly claim the defense of another. The threat of an impending terrorist attack threatens the lives of hundreds if not thousands of American citizens. Whether such a defense will be upheld depends on the specific context within which the interrogation decision is made. If an attack appears increasingly likely, but our intelligence services and armed forces cannot prevent it without the information from the interrogation of a specific individual, then the more likely it will appear that the conduct in question will be seen as necessary. If intelligence and other information support the conclusion that an attack is increasingly certain, then the necessity for the interrogation will be reasonable. The increasing certainty of an attack will also satisfy the imminence requirement. Finally, the fact that previous al Qaeda attacks have had as their aim the deaths of American citizens, and that evidence of other plots have had a similar goal in mind, would justify proportionality of interrogation methods designed to elicit information to prevent such deaths.

To be sure, this situation is different from the usual self-defense justification, and, indeed, it overlaps with elements of the necessity defense. Self-defense as usually discussed involves using force against an individual who is about to conduct the attack. In the current circumstances, however, an enemy combatant in detention does not himself present a threat of harm. He is not actually carrying out the attack; rather, he has participated in the planning and preparation for the attack, or merely has knowledge of the attack through his membership in the terrorist organization. Nonetheless, leading scholarly commentators believe that interrogation of such individuals using methods that might violate Section 2340A would be justified under the doctrine of self-defense, because the combatant by aiding and promoting the terrorist plot "has culpably caused the situation where someone might get hurt. If hurting him is the only means to prevent the death or injury of others put at risk by his actions, such torture should be permissible, and on the same basis that self-defense is permissible." Michael S. Moore, *Torture and the Balance of Evils*, 23 Israel L. Rev. 280, 323 (1989) (symposium on Israel's Landau Commission Report).[4] Thus, some commentators believe that by helping to create the threat of loss of life, terrorists become culpable for the threat even though they do not actually carry out the attack itself. They may be hurt in an interrogation because they are part of the mechanism that has set the attack in motion, *id.* at 323, just as is someone who feeds ammunition or targeting information to an attacker. Under the present circumstances, therefore, even though a detained enemy combatant may not be the exact attacker—he is not planting the bomb, or piloting a hijacked plane to kill civilians—he still may be harmed in self-defense if he has knowledge of future attacks because he has assisted in their planning and execution.

Further, we believe that a claim by an individual of the defense of another would be further supported by the fact that, in this case, the nation itself is under attack and has the right to self-defense. This fact can bolster and support an individual claim of self-defense in a prosecution, according to the teaching of the Supreme Court in *In re Neagle,* 135 U.S. 1 (1890). In that case, the State of California arrested and held deputy U.S. Marshal Neagle for shooting and killing the assailant of Supreme Court Justice Field. In granting the writ of habeas corpus for Neagle's release, the Supreme

[4] Moore distinguishes that case from one in which a person has information that could stop a terrorist attack, but who does not take a hand in the terrorist activity itself, such as an innocent person who learns of the attack from her spouse. Moore, 23 Israel L. Rev. at 324. Such individuals, Moore finds, would not be subject to the use of force in self-defense, although they might be under the doctrine of necessity.

Court did not rely alone upon the marshal's right to defend another or his right to self-defense. Rather, the Court found that Neagle, as an agent of the United States and of the executive branch, was justified in the killing because, in protecting Justice Field, he was acting pursuant to the executive branch's inherent constitutional authority to protect the United States government. *Id.* at 67 ("We cannot doubt the power of the president to take measures for the protection of a judge of one of the courts of the United States who, while in the discharge of the duties of his office, is threatened with a personal attack which may probably result in his death."). That authority derives, according to the Court, from the President's power under Article II to take care that the laws are faithfully executed. In other words, Neagle as a federal officer not only could raise self-defense or defense of another, but also could defend his actions on the ground that he was implementing the Executive Branch's authority to protect the United States government.

If the right to defend the national government can be raised as a defense in an individual prosecution, as *Neagle* suggests, then a government defendant, acting in his official capacity, should be able to argue that any conduct that arguably violated Section 2340A was undertaken pursuant to more than just individual self-defense or defense of another. In addition, the defendant could claim that he was fulfilling the Executive Branch's authority to protect the federal government, and the nation, from attack. The September 11 attacks have already triggered that authority, as recognized both under domestic and international law. Following the example of *In re Neagle*, we conclude that a government defendant may also argue that his conduct of an interrogation, if properly authorized, is justified on the basis of protecting the nation from attack.

There can be little doubt that the nation's right to self-defense has been triggered under our law. The Constitution announces that one of its purposes is "to provide for the common defense." U.S. Const., Preamble. Article I, § 8 declares that Congress is to exercise its powers to "provide for the common Defence." *See also* 2 Pub. Papers of Ronald Reagan 920, 921 (1988–89) (right of self-defense recognized by Article 51 of the U.N. Charter). The President has a particular responsibility and power to take steps to defend the nation and its people. *In re Neagle,* 135 U.S. at 64. *See also* U.S. Const., Article IV. § 4 ("The United States shall . . . protect [each of the States] against Invasion"). As Commander-in-Chief and Chief Executive, he may use the armed forces to protect the nation and its people. *See, e.g., United States v. Verdugo-Urquidez,* 494 U.S. 259, 273 (1990). And he may employ secret agents to aid in his work as Commander-in-Chief. *Totten v. United States,* 92 U.S. 105, 106 (1876). As the Supreme Court observed in *The Prize Cases,* 67 U.S. (2 Black) 635 (1862), in response to an armed attack on the United States "the President is not only authorized but bound to resist force by force . . . without waiting for any special legislative authority." *Id.* at 668. The September 11 events were a direct attack on the United States, and as we have explained above, the President has authorized the use of military force with the support of Congress.[5]

[5] While the President's constitutional determination alone is sufficient to justify the nation's resort to self-defense, it also bears noting that the right to self-defense is further recognized under international law. Article 51 of the U.N. Charter declares that "[n]othing in the present Charter shall impair the inherent right of individual or collective self-defense if an armed attack occurs against a Member of the United Nations until the Security Council has taken the measures necessary to maintain international peace and security." The attacks of September 11, 2001 clearly constitute an armed attack against the United States, and indeed were the latest in a long history of al Qaeda sponsored attacks against the United States. This conclusion was acknowledged by the United Nations Security Council on September 28, 2001, when it unanimously adopted Resolution 1373 explicitly "reaffirming the inherent right of individual and collective self-defence as recognized by the charter of the United Nations." This right of self-defense is a right to effective self-defense. In other words, the victim state has the right to use force against the aggressor who has initiated an "armed

As we have made clear in other opinions involving the war against al Qaeda, the nation's right to self-defense has been triggered by the events of September 11. If a government defendant were to harm an enemy combatant during an interrogation in a manner that might arguably violate Section 2340A, he would be doing so in order to prevent further attacks on the United States by the al Qaeda terrorist network. In that case, we believe that he could argue that his actions were justified by the executive branch's constitutional authority to protect the nation from attack. This national and international version of the right to self-defense could supplement and bolster the government defendant's individual right.

Conclusion

For the foregoing reasons, we conclude that torture as defined in and proscribed by Sections 2340–2340A, covers only extreme acts. Severe pain is generally of the kind difficult for the victim to endure. Where the pain is physical, it must be of an intensity akin to that which accompanies serious physical injury such as death or organ failure. Severe mental pain requires suffering not just at the moment of infliction but it also requires lasting psychological harm, such as seen in mental disorders like post-traumatic stress disorder. Additionally, such severe mental pain can arise only from the predicate acts listed in Section 2340. Because the acts inflicting torture are extreme, there is significant range of acts that though

---

attack" until the threat has abated. The United States, through its military and intelligence personnel, has a right recognized by Article 51 to continue using force until such time as the threat posed by al Qaeda and other terrorist groups connected to the September 11th attacks is completely ended" Other treaties reaffirm the right of the United States to use force in its self-defense. See, e.g., Inter-American Treaty of Reciprocal Assistance, art. 3, Sept. 2, 1947, T.I.A.S. No. 1838, 21 U.N.T.S. 77 (Rio Treaty); North Atlantic Treaty, art. 5, Apr. 4, 1949, 63 Stat 2241, 34 U.N.T.S. 243.

they might constitute cruel, inhuman, or degrading treatment or punishment fail to rise to the level of torture.

Further, we conclude that under the circumstances of the current war against al Qaeda and its allies, application of Section 2340A to interrogations undertaken pursuant to the President's Commander-in-Chief powers may be unconstitutional. Finally, even if an interrogation method might violate Section 2340A, necessity or self-defense could provide justifications that would eliminate any criminal liability.

Please let us know if we can be of further assistance.

Jay S. Bybee
Assistant Attorney General

Donald Rumsfeld Testimony Before the House Armed Services Committee

In the testimony below, during a House Armed Services Committee hearing on May 7, 2004, Donald Rumsfeld attempts to defend interrogation tactics by asserting that they were "a very different thing from softening up."

REP. SPRATT: One of the recommendations [General Miller] made was that the Joint Task Force should create a guard team that, quote, "sets the conditions for the successful interrogation and exploitation of detainees." Exploitation. Later on, General Taguba and General Ryder made an examination or an assessment, and they said, according to the Taguba report, the recommendation of General Miller's team that the guard force be actively engaged in setting conditions for successful exploitation of the internees appears to be in conflict with the recommendation of General Ryder's team and AR 190-8, that military police do not, quote, "participate in military intelligence," supervise interrogation sessions. Moreover, military police should not be involved with setting favorable conditions for subsequent interviews.

Now they were implying that he had sanctioned this activity and that this activity was wrong for a reason. And I think the reason is you may get your MPs involved in the wrong kind of activity, or they may, without adequate supervision, go beyond what is approved procedure. General Miller is now in charge of detainee operations in Iraq. Has any correction been issued to him, or has any exception been taken for sanctioning these kind of policies?

SEC. RUMSFELD: I'll let General Smith respond in a minute, but first let me—you used some correct quotes from the assessment by Miller and by the Tagubu—Taguba—

excuse me, Taguba report, that seem in conflict. What was found at Guantánamo was that the task was to do three things. One was to keep terrorists off the street so they don't go kill more innocent men, women and children; and the second was to look at punishment and potential prosecution of people; and the third task was to interrogate and learn about additional terrorist acts that might be conducted so we could save the lives of American people.

The tasks are different for the people who have the responsibility for the custody of the detainee. Their job is to have them safe and secure and off the street. The interrogators' job is to learn what they can learn from them to save other lives. It is quite proper, in my view, and in my understanding of this—indeed, it is desirable—to have the people who keep them safe and secure do it in a manner that allows the interrogation process to be the most effective.

And I can see where the words from one assessment report and the words from the Taguba report being different—that one could raise that issue. And that is clearly something that we need to address and come to some conclusions on. But I don't think that necessarily, on the face of it, there's a problem.

(To General Smith.) And do you know if there was any corrections issued, as the question was—

REP. SPRATT: Are you saying, then, that this policy of loosening up said that the MPs should be engaged in this procedure of loosening up, setting up, and preparing the prisoners for interrogation and, quote, "exploitation"?

SEC. RUMSFELD: Of course not. The things you're quoting about softening up—

REP. SPRATT: Yeah.

SEC. RUMSFELD:—I saw that myself. Of course not. That is not the policy or the procedure. What—

REP. SPRATT: And you said—but it appears in General Miller's assessment, that they should set the conditions for successful interrogation and exploitation of internees and set the conditions—

SEC. RUMSFELD: That is a very different thing from softening up, I would submit.[3]

Later in the same testimony, Rumsfeld seems to indicate a belief that the application of the Geneva Conventions to the interrogation of detainees is flexible, depending on whether the detainee is considered "high-value" or "low-level."

SEC. RUMSFELD: In terms of the Geneva Convention, on the other hand, there is a difference in this sense: that the high-value targets become much more interesting from the standpoint of the interrogation process, whereas a simple low-level person is simply being kept off the street for a period.[4]

Alberto Gonzales Op-Ed

In this passage from his May 15, 2004, op-ed in the New York Times, *Counsel to the President Gonzales argues explicitly that al Qaeda is not protected by the Geneva Conventions.*

"Geneva establishes protections for combatants who fight on behalf of states that have agreed to comply with the conventions and who distinguish themselves from civilians. That, in part, is how one earns prisoner-of-war status. According that status to terrorists who hide among civilian populations and viciously flout the core Geneva principle of protecting the innocent would provide a perverse incentive to terrorists to continue to operate in violation of the laws of war."[5]

5

The Center for Constitutional Rights Rebuttal to the Memos and the Torture Program: Illegal Before 9/11, Still Illegal Today

"This war is distinctive and will be remembered because we, as a nation, despite our laws, values and traditions, consciously applied cruelty against captive individuals, and sought to amend where we interpret our laws so as to make this, which used to be illegal, legal."

—Alberto Mora, retired general counsel of the U.S. Navy, keynote address at the International Law Symposium, "International Law at a Crossroads," February 23, 2007

This rebuttal is divided into three sections: the first section explains why none of the defendants can rely on the erroneous legal memos that attempt to legalize, justify, and authorize torture. The second focuses on what we are calling "illegal lawyering" and why the defendant lawyers are criminally liable for aiding and abetting torture by their writing of legal opinions authorizing torture. And the final section argues that the individual defendants who authorized or supervised torture and war crimes are criminally responsible for the torture program and war crimes.

I. Defendants Cannot Rely on the Erroneous Legal Memos

The defendants in this case rely entirely on the legal claim that what they call "coercive interrogations" or "enhanced interrogation techniques"—and what we prosecutors call torture—did not violate the law. They do not dispute the facts of the interrogations or the "techniques" that were applied to detainees. Their argument is that such techniques did not violate the criminal law of the United States. They say this despite U.S. criminal laws that prohibit violations of the Geneva Conventions, war crimes, and torture.

You might ask yourself, how this can be? How can it be that there are laws that prohibit torture and war crimes and yet the defendants can argue they are not guilty?

The defendants' answer is that the post-9/11 legal memos demonstrate that their conduct was not criminal. The heart of their defense is that what most legal scholars and courts believed was torture prior to 9/11 was no longer torture after 9/11, that the Geneva Conventions could not be violated because they had no application to the post-9/11 detainees, and that no matter what the law said, the president could ignore the law and torture people in the name of national security.

None of these legal positions of the defendants reflect the law. The memos were written to change the law and avoid its prohibitions. While it may be that the lower-level soldier or agent who relied on this erroneous legal advice has a possible legal defense (and only in exceptional and limited circumstances), that is not true for the higher-ups. Rumsfeld and others (including the lawyers who wrote the memos) were part of a conspiracy or common scheme to facilitate and aid and abet torture. It is these defendants in front of you who were part of the plan to torture. The memos were written as part of that torture plan with the full consciousness that the conclusions were contrary to clearly established law and would be used to allow torture.

You can compare the way the defendants approached the prohibitions on torture to the ways a particularly creative tax lawyer might treat the tax code and find every possible loophole. Instead of striving to uphold what we thought were our country's moral principles, the defendants sought to exploit every loophole they could find or manufacture. But that analogy is too kind to the defendants. They were not exploiting and finding loopholes; they were writing legal opinions that were unwarranted and clearly contrary to law. Opinions analogous to these in the tax context would have ensured the jailing of those lawyers engaged in their writing. The memos here were written with the consciousness that the legal conclusions they espoused were to be applied to the interrogations of hundreds, if not thousands, of detainees. They were written to immunize those who authorized and engaged in torture from being prosecuted. You must see this case for what it is: the efforts of the defendants to establish a torture program in the United States and around the world. And they succeeded. But they can be stopped. It is your job to hold them accountable for their actions and not let them try and hide behind manufactured legal opinions that they knew to be false and utterly without merit.

The problem for these defendants was that U.S. law prohibited torture and war crimes and to get people to torture they needed to try and persuade the would-be torturers that they would not be prosecuted. So they, and by they, we mean all of the defendants, hatched the scheme to manufacture utterly fallacious legal opinions allowing torture that they hoped would provide a defense for them in case of prosecution. But as is demonstrated below, their efforts are to no avail. The principle arguments made in their defense are four:

First, that the Geneva Conventions did not apply to the war in Afghanistan, the Taliban, or al Qaeda, and if they did not apply, the war crimes statute, which makes Geneva violations crimes, had no applicability.

Second, that even if the Geneva Conventions applied, the president, as commander-in-chief, had the authority to suspend the Conventions.

Third, that the Convention Against Torture's prohibition on torture was to be read narrowly so as to prohibit only acts that inflict pain equivalent to major organ failure or death.

Fourth, that the president can override the Constitution, laws, and treaties that prohibit torture.

None of these so-called defenses has any merit.

First Argument

As the Supreme Court reaffirmed in its 2006 decision in *Hamdan v. Rumsfeld*, the Geneva Conventions do apply to detainees held in the so-called "war on terror." This was not a novel Supreme Court finding; the law has always been that every human being detained under the laws of war is protected at a minimum by the humane treatment provisions of Geneva.

Defendants had concluded otherwise to protect themselves from criminal prosecution and not because they had valid legal reasons for doing so. Defendant Gonzales in a January 25, 2002, memo to President Bush explained: "It is difficult to predict the motives of prosecutors and independent counsels who may in the future decide to pursue unwarranted charges based on Section 2241 [of the War Crimes Act]."[1] He continued that a presidential decision not to apply Geneva Conventions "would provide a solid defense to any future prosecution." Put simply, their argument was this: if the Geneva Conventions do not apply, then at least there is no violation of the War Crimes Statute for torture and inhumane treatment, as only violations of Geneva are within its language. This is the primary reason the memos by defendants Yoo and Bybee spend pages laying out arcane, bizarre, and fallacious reasoning in trying to establish that the Geneva Conventions do not apply. To come to these conclusions, the defendants deliberately ignored key precedents, including more than a dozen Supreme Court cases. They also ignored the Vienna Convention on the Law of Treaties, which provides that "provisions relating to the protection of the human person contained in treaties of a humanitarian character [i.e. the Geneva Conventions]" cannot be suspended.[2]

John Yoo's January 9, 2002, memo also argued that the Geneva Conventions do not apply to either al Qaeda or Taliban soldiers. Yoo explicitly framed his analysis in the context of the U.S. War Crimes Act, which creates criminal liability for certain violations of the Geneva Conventions and other laws of war.[3] Again, it must be seen as an effort to avoid prosecution so that torture could be carried out unhampered by law.

Defendant Yoo claimed that al Qaeda is a nonstate actor that has not signed the Geneva Conventions, and that thus the United States is not bound to apply the Conventions to al Qaeda.[4] As to the Taliban, Yoo claimed that while Afghanistan had been a party to the Geneva Conventions in the past, the country should now be treated as a "failed state" with no actual functioning government.[5] The Taliban regime should thus be treated as a militia or movement, but not as a state that could fulfill its obligations under Geneva.[6]

Through this reasoning, Yoo claimed that no provision of the Geneva Conventions applies to either al Qaeda or the Taliban. Yoo's argument is especially shocking in that the decision not to abide by Geneva represents a major break with fifty years of U.S. conduct.

Defendant Yoo's legal reasoning about the Taliban and Afghanistan is seriously flawed. Specifically, the United Nations Security Council never failed to recognize Afghanistan as a state, and it specifically said that the laws of war, and more specifically the Geneva Conventions, were to be applied in Afghanistan, before and after the U.S. 2001 military intervention (see Resolution 1378 of September 14, 2001). The Security Council urged the Afghan forces to "adhere strictly to their obligations" arising from the laws of war, which shows that the Taliban regime was recognized as a government engaged in war and bound by the Geneva Conventions.[7]

For al Qaeda, according to the laws of war, even though its fighters are not recognized as prisoners of war (POWs) because they were not part of a nation state, they are entitled to at least the core protections of Common Article 3, found in all the Geneva Conventions, which provides for the "minimum" each party to the Conventions is "bound" to and which includes the prohibition of cruel or inhuman treatment and torture in all situations.

This application of the humane treatment provisions of Geneva was argued point by point by lawyers inside the State Department at the time of these memos, and the military heavily criticized the Yoo memo.[8] A January 11, 2002, memo from the legal adviser of the State Department, William Taft IV, to Yoo stated that "both the most important factual assumptions on which [the] draft [memorandum] is based and its legal analysis are seriously flawed."[9]

Second Argument

There is no merit to the claim that the president has the authority to suspend the Geneva Conventions and to the claim that Common Article 3 of those Conventions, and especially its humane treatment protections, has no applicability to the detainees. Defendant Yoo argued that even if Afghanistan is still a party to the Conventions, the president has the authority to suspend the Conventions either as retaliation for alleged breaches of the laws of war by the Taliban or because Afghanistan "lacked the capacity to fulfill its treaty obligations."

Defendant Yoo is simply wrong to assert that the president can suspend portions of the Conventions as a reprisal for acts committed by opposing fighters. Indeed, the Vienna Conventions on the Law of Treaties—ratified by the United States—specifically and unambiguously states that "provisions relating to the protection of the human person contained in treaties of a humanitarian character [i.e., the Geneva Conventions], in particular to provisions prohibiting any form of reprisals against persons protected by such treaties" cannot be suspended.[10] The fact that Yoo chose not to mention this binding provision was also stressed by State Department officials and academics as a flagrant omission in Yoo's argument.

It is likewise with Common Article 3, which prohibits torture and cruel treatment of civilians and unlawful combatants (such as combatants who dress in civilian clothing while engaging in armed attacks or terrorist groups). It cannot be deemed inapplicable to anyone, not even by the president: it applies everywhere. Thus, Yoo was out on an undeniable legal limb in his attempts to restrict Article 3's application. His argument was based on the erroneous conclusion that Afghanistan was a failed state and is therefore no longer considered a contracting party. On this basis he concludes that Common Article 3 does not apply altogether. However, as we have seen, Afghanistan was never considered a failed state by the international community and it *is* a contracting party to the Conventions, rendering this argument absurd.

Defendant Yoo is incorrect in stating that Common Article 3 strictly applies only to internal armed conflicts in a state and therefore would not protect al Qaeda. In the case of al Qaeda fighters, Common Article 3, which constitutes a safety net of basic fundamental rights, does apply since it is binding on any state party to the Conventions fighting anyone anywhere in the world. *No person anywhere in the world is outside of basic human rights protections.* Common Article 3 has long since become customary international law and is widely held to apply to all wars, including international and noninternational armed conflicts.[11] Defendant Yoo thus grossly misstated the law when he asserted that Common Article 3 of the Geneva Conventions did not apply.

Defendants' erroneous legal advice and ignoring of the Geneva Conventions must be seen in light of a similar situation that occurred in Germany during WWII. General Marshal Wilhelm Keitel was the German Chief of Staff of the High Command of the Armed Forces. He was tried and condemned in 1945 before the International Military Tribunal in Nuremberg.[12] He had denied Russian soldiers the Geneva Law of War's protections—he refused to give them prisoner-of-war status. Keitel stated that the Geneva Conventions were *obsolete*. Likewise, defendant Alberto Gonzales, in his January 25, 2002, memorandum asserted that the "new paradigm" of the "war on terror" makes certain provisions of the Geneva Conventions "quaint" and "renders *obsolete*" the "strict limitations on questioning of enemy prisoners."

In an article in the *Los Angeles Times*, attorney Scott Horton explained that Keitel's remark was "remembered by U.S. prosecutors, who cited it as an aggravating circumstance in seeking, and obtaining, the death penalty" against him.[13] While we do not advocate for the death penalty against anyone, this does demonstrate the seriousness with which Gonzales's and other defendants' ignoring of the Geneva Conventions should be taken.

President Bush's memo of February 7, 2002, following defendant Yoo's January 9, 2002, memo, suspended the Geneva Conventions for al Qaeda and denied POW status to members of the Taliban.[14] The memo also stated that the military should treat detainees "humanely and, to the extent appropriate and consistent with military necessity, in a manner consistent with the principle of Geneva."[15] This "military necessity" exception meant that the military could completely avoid applying any of the Geneva standards to the detainees. However, states cannot simply create "necessity" exceptions to core provisions of the Conventions, especially those that conflict with the very purpose of the Conventions themselves. Torture is never permitted and military necessity, whatever that means, is not an exception to its absolute ban.

Third Argument

In the infamous so-called "torture memo" of August 1, 2002, authored by defendants Bybee and Yoo, written at the behest of defendant Addington and addressed to and approved by defendant Gonzales, the legal definition of torture was narrowed so that age-old torture techniques such as waterboarding could be authorized. According to the memo, if the victim was caused bodily pain, it would only constitute torture if the pain was "equivalent in intensity to the pain accompanying serious physical injury, such as organ failure, impairment of bodily function, or even death." As a result of this memo, torture techniques were described as not punishable.

The Yoo and Bybee torture memo was not an abstract legal memo. It was written to address Vice President Cheney's concerns that the CIA was unwilling to interrogate alleged al Qaeda suspects, such as Abu Zubayadh, in a sufficiently harsh manner, and to overcome the CIA's opposition to techniques that it believed violated the Convention Against Torture. It was written with the knowledge that its conclusions would be used to harshly treat detainees and employ techniques such as waterboarding.

Defendants Bybee and Yoo wrote that "torture is not the mere infliction of pain or suffering on another . . . The victim must experience intense pain or suffering of the kind that is equivalent to the pain that would be associated with serious physical injury so severe that death, organ failure, or permanent damage resulting in a loss of significant body function will likely result."[16] This was clearly wrong and against established law.

The notion of "severe pain" employed in the memo is taken from statutes providing the circumstances under which patients are entitled to emergency health benefits—a situation irrelevant to the definition of torture.[17] It was this definition that was employed instead of the definition used in treaties, statutes, and court decisions that have defined torture.

In December 2004, more than two years after the torture memo, the Justice Department's Office of Legal Counsel issued a new memo on torture superseding the August 1, 2002, memo[18] and stressing that the statutes referred to in the August memo were irrelevant to the question of torture and did not "provide a proper guide for interpreting "severe pain" in the very different context of the prohibition against torture in sections 2340–2340A."[19]

Nor does the Convention Against Torture (CAT) "prohibit only the worst forms of cruel, inhuman, or degrading treatment or punishment."[20] The U.S. State Department itself confirmed this view in its 1999 Initial Report to the U.N. Committee Against Torture.[21] The prohibition of cruel, inhuman, or degrading treatment is just as absolute as it is for torture, and criminal liability arises in both situations. The CAT also does not categorize cruel, inhuman, or degrading treatment, meaning that Bybee and Yoo's reference to the "worst forms of cruel, inhuman, or degrading treatment" is utterly baseless. There is no cruel, inhuman, or degrading treatment that is legal.

Moreover, many cruel and degrading acts become torture depending on their severity, duration, and their use in combination with other acts. The U.N. Committee against Torture, the U.N. body of independent experts that implement the Convention Against Torture, has considered that the following interrogation techniques constitute cruel, inhuman, or degrading treatment under the Convention, but also torture, which is, the committee concluded, "particularly evident where such methods of interrogation are used in combination": restraining in very painful conditions; hooding under special conditions; sounding of loud music for prolonged periods; sleep deprivation for prolonged periods; threats, including death threats; violent shaking; and extreme temperatures.[22]

The relevance of such findings—that these interrogation techniques constitute torture and cruel, inhuman, or degrading treatment, especially when used in combination—was especially important, as these are precisely the methods used by the United States in the context of the "war on terror." Yet, defendants Bybee and Yoo chose to ignore these precedents. In 2004, the importance of this finding was stressed again by the then–United Nations Special Rapporteur on Torture and Other Forms of Cruel, Inhuman, or Degrading Treatment or Punishment, Theo van Boven, who reaffirmed that these specific methods used to secure information from suspected terrorists were illegal as they constituted torture and cruel, inhuman, or degrading treatment.

In addition to the CAT, the Geneva Conventions and human rights law also prohibit "violence," threats of violence, "cruel" treatment, "physical and moral coercion . . . to obtain information," "physical suffering," "inhuman" treatment, "degrading" treatment, "humiliating" treatment, and "intimidation" during interrogation.[23] Moreover, as stated earlier, the United States also ratified the International Covenant on Civil and Political Rights, which equally condemns both torture *and* "cruel, inhuman, or degrading treatment or punishment."

The torture memo became the basis for the CIA's use of extreme interrogation methods. Essentially, it became Department of Defense interrogation policy—interrogation techniques approved by Donald Rumsfeld and employed at Guantánamo, and confirmed in his order of December 2, 2002, were precisely shaped by the torture memo. Because it was clearly written to give legal cover to those who illegally violated the Geneva Conventions, and its legal conclusions are unwarranted, it becomes more than abstract legal advice. It becomes a knowing act in the criminal conspiracy to aid and abet torture. Lawyers cannot purposely give unwarranted legal opinions that they know or suspect will be employed to carry out unlawful acts.

Legal scholars considered the conclusions of the torture memo to be entirely without merit, false, bizarre, and written to authorize techniques that run afoul of the CAT ratified by the United States. The torture memo was written by defendants Bybee and Yoo in blatant violation of the most basic law standards, resulting in a document that Yale Law School Dean Harold Koh, in his testimony before the U.S. Senate, condemned:

> The August 1, 2002, Bybee Opinion is a stain upon our law and our national reputation. A legal opinion that is so lacking in historical context, that offers a definition of torture so narrow that it would have exculpated Saddam Hussein, that reads the Commander-in-Chief power so as to remove Congress as a check against torture, that turns Nuremberg on its head, and that gives government officials a license for cruelty can only be described—as my predecessor, Dean Eugene Rostow of Yale Law School, described the Japanese internment cases—as a "disaster."[24]

Fourth Argument

There is no merit to the claim that the Constitution, federal statues, and treaties that prohibit torture can be overridden by the president's claimed constitutional power to conduct a military campaign. By essentially stating that the president can authorize torture, the August 1, 2002, memo itself flouted the U.S. Constitution. Under the Constitution, the president must faithfully execute the laws, which include treaty law, customary international law, and, of course, the Constitution itself. For instance, the memo failed to mention that the Constitution grants to Congress the powers to define "offences against the Law of Nations," which strengthens the argument that Congress has the power to ban torture. Moreover, the memo's reading of the commander-in-chief power contravenes the Fifth and Eighth

Amendments of the U.S. Constitution. Koh rightfully stressed: "[T]he Eighth Amendment does not say 'nor [shall] cruel and unusual punishments [be] inflicted' except when the Commander-in-Chief orders, and the Fifth Amendment's Due Process Clause nowhere sanctions executive torture."[25]

The memo also plainly disregarded international law, which clearly states that heads of state may never, under any circumstance, authorize the use of torture and cruel, inhuman, or degrading treatment. Theo van Boven recalled that:

> No executive, legislative, administrative or judicial measure authorizing recourse to torture and cruel, inhuman or degrading treatment or punishment can be considered as lawful under international law and, therefore, any measure of that kind would engage the State's responsibility, whether it be an act of torture directly committed by, or at the instigation of, or with the consent or acquiescence of a public official or any other person acting in an official capacity on behalf of that State. A head of State, also in his or her capacity as commander-in-chief, should therefore not authorize his or her subordinates to use torture, or guarantee immunity to the authors and co-authors of and accomplices to torture. The argument that public officials have used torture having been advised by lawyers or experts that their actions were permissible is not acceptable either. No special circumstance may be invoked to justify a violation of the prohibition of torture for any reason, including an order from a superior officer or a public authority.

The memo also simply failed to mention a key precedent, *Youngstown Sheet & Tube Co. v. Sawyer*, which is the leading Supreme Court case on separation of powers regarding executive power in a time of crisis.[26] In *Youngstown*, the justices rejected the argument that President Truman had an inherent constitutional power to seize private steel mills to prevent a strike during the

Korean War, the best-known instance of an American president attempting to put himself above the Constitution in the name of national security.

Unfortunately, nothing has truly improved within the Bush administration. In October 2007, the *New York Times* revealed that a series of secret memos and legal opinions approved by defendant former Attorney General Gonzales in 2005 explicitly authorized U.S. interrogators to use a combination of brutal interrogation techniques including the use of extreme cold and head slapping, and, for the first time, waterboarding was explicitly authorized.

The United Nations Committee Against Torture, in its July 25, 2006, Conclusions and Recommendations to the United States of America, said it "remains concerned at the absence of clear legal provisions ensuring that the Convention's prohibition against torture is not derogated from under any circumstances, in particular since 11 September 2001."[27] It added:

> The State party [The United States] should also ensure that any interrogation rules, instructions or methods do not derogate from the principle of absolute prohibition of torture and that no doctrine under domestic law impedes the full criminal responsibility of perpetrators of acts of torture. . . . The State party [The United States] should rescind any interrogation technique, including methods involving sexual humiliation, "waterboarding," "short-shackling" and using dogs to induce fear, that constitutes torture or cruel, inhuman or degrading treatment or punishment, in all places of detention under its de facto effective control, in order to comply with its obligations under the Convention.

But the Bush administration has not yet shown any sign of a change of policy and continues to torture.

II. Illegal Lawyering: The Defendant Lawyers Are Criminally Liable for Aiding and Abetting Torture

The defendants who wrote these memos gave practical and substantial assistance and encouragement to those committing the crime of torture. Through these memos, the Bush administration's lawyers aided the commission of torture and cruel, inhuman, or degrading treatment, and violations of the humanitarian protections of the Geneva Conventions. It was not only foreseeable that the legal positions taken in these memos would lead to such crimes; it was the very purpose of these defendants in writing these memos. Without these opinions, the torture program would not have occurred.

The Bush administration's lawyers should therefore be found personally criminally liable for having aided and abetted torture and war crimes. There is no question that lawyers can be liable criminally if they knowingly give unwarranted and false legal advice in situations where it is foreseeable that death or serious harm to people will result from that advice. It would not be the first time lawyers are found responsible for such crimes.

While it may be unusual for lawyers giving legal advice to be charged with complicity in war crimes, it is not unprecedented. The key decision upholding this principle is the World War II Nuremberg case *United States v. Altstoetter*, known as the "Justice Case."[28] The legal principles of liability underlying the *Altstoetter* case are well known and not in dispute. The defendants in that case included Nazi government lawyers who were found criminally liable for drafting memoranda and decrees that justified and led to war crimes. American prosecutor Telford Taylor labeled them a "dishonor to their profession"; the lawyers were "called to account for violating constitutional guaranties or withholding due process of law," and indicted for participating in international crimes through the abuse of the judicial and penal process, resulting, among other crimes, in acts of torture.[29] The tribunal stated:

> The charge, in brief, is that of conscious participation in a nationwide governmentally organized system of cruelty and injustice, in violation of the laws of war and of humanity, and perpetrated in the name of law by the authority of the Ministry of Justice.

The Nuremberg judges famously concluded:

> The prostitution of a judicial system for the accomplishment of criminal ends involves an element of evil to the State which is not found in frank atrocities which do not sully judicial robes.[30]

To be found guilty under this standard, it was necessary to prove that specific actions taken by the individual defendants furthered the plan to perpetrate the crime. This was further elaborated on as a need to show that the defendant "consciously participated in the plan or took a consenting part therein" to further the abuses.

The equivalent crime in today's world is "aiding and abetting." Under the most stringent standard employed at the United Nations International Criminal Tribunal for ex-Yugoslavia (ICTY), there is criminal responsibility for aiding and abetting where the defendant has engaged in acts that provide the principal with "practical assistance, encouragement, or moral support which has a substantial effect on the perpetration of the crime." The Trial Chamber of the ICTY has strongly advocated applying criminal liability to all individuals who participate in state torture. It has proclaimed that:

> the nature of the crime and the forms that it takes, as well as the intensity of international condemnation of torture, suggest that in the case of torture all those who in some

degree participate in the crime and in particular take part in the pursuance of one of its underlying purposes, are equally liable.[31]

There is no question that lawyers can be liable criminally if they knowingly give unwarranted and false legal advice in situations in which it is foreseeable that death or serious harm to people will result from that advice. Defendants Yoo, Bybee, Gonzales, Addington, and Haynes authored and authorized memos designed to facilitate the use of more brutal interrogation techniques by assuring that no criminal prosecution for torture or war crimes would follow. They gave false legal advice, failing to mention key precedents, of which any reasonable attorney would have been aware. This was more than bad lawyering, this was aiding and abetting their clients' violation of the law by justifying the commission of a crime using false legal rhetoric.

These memos remain, today, the prevailing legal justifications for the ongoing torture of those held by the CIA, while President George W. Bush, as recently as October 5, 2007, repeatedly claims "this government does not torture." Yet, these memos can in no way provide a legal cover to the high-ranking civilian and military officials who have authorized, implemented, or supervised the illegal interrogation techniques used on detainees. These officials must be held individually criminally responsible under U.S. and international law.

The writing and promulgation of the Bush administration's memos cannot go unpunished. They were written by high-level attorneys in a context in which the opinions represented the governing law and were to be employed by the president in setting detainee policy. The defendants knew the legal conclusions were to be applied to the interrogations of hundreds or thousands of detainees.

The defendants who wrote these memos gave practical and substantial assistance and encouragement to those committing the crime of torture. They aided and abetted torture; cruel, inhuman, or degrading treatment; and violations of the humanitarian protections of the Geneva Conventions. It was not only foreseeable that the legal positions taken in these memos would lead to such crimes; it was the very purpose of the defendants when they wrote these memos.

For these reasons, Defendants Gonzales, Yoo, Bybee, Addington, and Haynes must be held personally accountable for aiding and abetting acts of torture.

III. Defendants Who Authorized or Supervised Torture and War Crimes Are Criminally Responsible

Under international law, individual criminal responsibility based on membership in a criminal group is analyzed by way of analogy to conspiracy. Both involve cooperation for criminal purposes. The person must have knowingly and voluntarily joined the group or have been personally implicated in the commission of criminal acts. In this case, it is not difficult to prove how all fourteen defendants cited here conspired to perpetrate acts of torture. The government lawyers were only one of various means to implement the torture program, the memos being part of the common plan to commit a crime—this is partly why these memos cannot possibly provide a cover against criminal liability.

The Appeals Chamber of the International Criminal Tribunal for ex-Yugoslavia (ICTY) has set forth in a case decided in 2002 at the Hague the common purpose doctrine—or "joint criminal enterprise" doctrine. It has stated that:

> A joint criminal enterprise exists where there is an understanding or arrangement amounting to an agreement between two or more persons that they will commit a crime. The understanding or arrangement need not be express, and its existence

may be inferred from all the circumstances. It need not have been reached at any time before the crime is committed. The circumstances in which two or more persons are participating together in the commission of a particular crime may themselves establish an unspoken understanding or arrangement amounting to an agreement formed between them then and there to commit that crime.[32]

This category of responsibility is based on an analysis of national case law, especially from the American and British military war crimes tribunals. The ICTY considers that responsibility exists as soon as the risk of the crime being committed "became a predictable consequence of the execution of the common plan."[33] The objective elements required to assess common purpose liability, according to the tribunal are: 1) the plurality of persons, 2) a common plan, design, or purpose which amounts to or involves that commission of a crime, and 3) participation, which may be in the form of assistance in, or contribution to, the execution of the common plan or purpose, rather than the commission of a specific crime.

In addition, it is well established under international law that individual criminal responsibility is not limited to persons who have directly committed a crime by personally perpetrating its material elements. Civilian superiors and military commanders of the direct perpetrators of crimes are to be held equally liable for the crimes that they have not personally committed but for which they are nevertheless responsible. They are responsible for their own actions that have directly triggered or caused the commission of a crime, such as ordering, soliciting, and aiding and abetting it. They can also be held liable if they failed to prevent their subordinates from committing crimes and failed to punish them. This general principle of individual criminal responsibility has been recognized by national courts for centuries, and international law has followed this path.

In fact, the individual who orders an international crime such as torture "is not a mere accomplice but rather a perpetrator by means, using a subordinate to commit the crime."[34] Responsibility for ordering a crime requires the individual to be in a position of authority and to have used that authority to instruct a subordinate to commit an offense. What matters is that the order was given "with the awareness of the substantial likelihood that a crime will be committed in the execution of that order."[35] And criminal responsibility arises even when the crimes are executed subsequently by lower-rank officials or even soldiers, whether or not the order had been personally given to them.

For a government to issue secret internal memos reversing decades of precedents and clearly established law, and ignoring national legislation and international obligations, the very idea that those memos would be sufficient to avoid criminal prosecution for torture does not make sense. Countries that are a party to fundamental treaties such as the Geneva Conventions and the Convention Against Torture cannot claim that they are no longer under the obligation to abide by them. Above all, the prohibition against torture is a *jus cogens* norm, meaning that because the international community has accepted that this is one of the most severe crimes that can ever be committed, no circumstances may *ever* justify the recourse to torture—and this is a binding rule. In other words, no national legislation allowing torture can be regarded as valid, and therefore internal governmental memos cannot legally allow it, or provide any type of legal cover for those implementing it.

Van Boven, the former U.N. Special Rapporteur on Torture, reiterated in his 2004 report to the U.N. General Assembly this absolute prohibition against torture and all other forms of ill treatment, in all circumstances, even when facing terrorism—which includes, he specified, situations in which the government is attempting to obtain intelligence value from suspected terrorists.

The military defendants in this case, up to and including Donald Rumsfeld, established the torture program, authorized torture, created an environment conducive to torture by demanding "more actionable" intelligence, and failed to punish those who committed torture and thereby prevent further abuses.

The torture at Abu Ghraib occurred in the immediate aftermath of a decision by Defendant Rumsfeld to step up the hunt for "actionable intelligence" among Iraqi prisoners. He authorized the techniques to be used and sent General Miller from Guantánamo to Iraq to "Gitmoize" it. The Schlesinger Report noted, "It is clear that pressures for additional intelligence and the more aggressive methods sanctioned by the Secretary of Defense memorandum, resulted in stronger interrogation techniques that were believed to be needed and appropriate in the treatment of detainees defined as 'unlawful combatants.'"[36] In other words, if you disregard the euphemisms, Rumsfeld wanted and got torture.

As then-Secretary of Defense, defendant Rumsfeld was the penultimate civilian commander over the military, after President Bush. There is no doubt Rumsfeld had control over the individuals who committed war crimes. He personally ordered the commission of acts constituting war crimes and torture, and set the conditions possible for the commission of others.

As the highest civilian and military official in charge, it was the defendant's personal responsibility to ensure all military and civilian personnel acted within the confines of the law and he knew that the law was not reflected in the memos and that those memos were only there as a possible protection against his own future prosecution. Defendants were also perfectly aware of the possibility that more crimes beyond those they approved or supervised would be committed, and they failed to take any measure to prevent this from happening, which led to exactly what they had illegally planned for: the widespread mistreatment of detainees in a torture program.

For all the reasons stated above, we submit that fourteen defendants are guilty of war crimes and crimes of torture, for having ordered, authorized, and aided and abetted torture and for having failed to prevent and punish acts of torture perpetrated against detainees held in Guantánamo, in Abu Ghraib, and in the many other U.S.-controlled detention centers in Iraq, in Afghanistan, and in secret sites around the world. We trust that you, the reader, will find them guilty of these crimes.

6

Exhibits: Photos from Guantánamo and Abu Ghraib

Former Guantánamo detainees, the Tipton Three.

Detainees at Guantánamo during the first days.

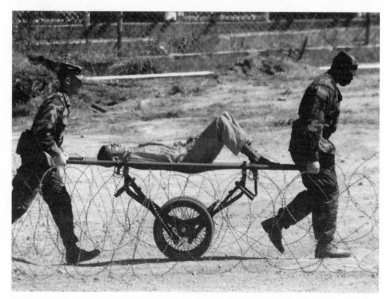

MPs transport a detainee to an interrogation room at camp X-Ray in February 2002.

In this AP photo from March 2002, detainees at camp X-Ray pray in their cells.

Two naked and hooded detainees are made to simulate oral sex in Abu Ghraib. On many occasions, Iraqi prisoners were put in degrading and humiliating sexual situations, such as being made to masturbate in public or being sodomized.

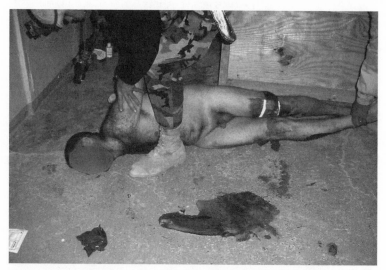

A bleeding Iraqi detainee is restrained on the ground by two soldiers. It is possible that his injuries were from dog bites, as the use of dogs as an intimidation tactic was a frequent interrogation method at Abu Ghraib.

An unidentified U.S. soldier holds back an unmuzzled dog that has cornered a frightened Iraqi detainee. Although "acts of violence or intimidation" are prohibited in the U.S. Army's field manual, a plan approved by U.S. intelligence personnel allowed the use of unmuzzled dogs during interrogations to frighten and intimidate detainees.

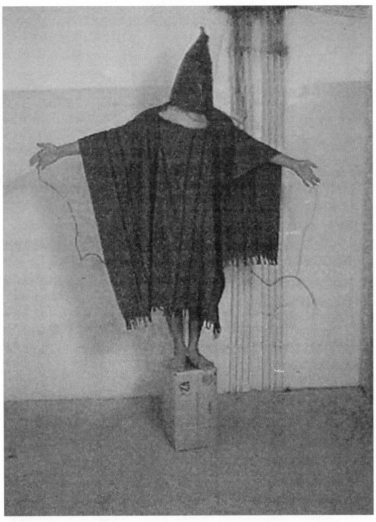

In what is perhaps the most well-known Abu Ghraib photo, a detainee nicknamed "Gilligan" by soldiers at Abu Ghraib is made to stand on a box with wires attached to his hands. He was told that if he fell off, he would be electrocuted.

Epilogue

7

Prosecuting War Crimes

The Center for Constitutional Rights's case against Donald Rumsfeld and other officials is not the first of its kind—it is merely the latest in a series of legal challenges stemming from the post-World War II trials at Nuremberg, that have attempted to hold officials accountable for crimes against humanity. All of these cases, exemplified by the case against Chilean dictator Augusto Pinochet chronicled in this chapter, make use of the legal theory of universal jurisdiction, which states that any state government can prosecute officials from any other country if the crimes they have committed are of such magnitude as to become international affairs.

We end with the story of the Center for Constitutional Rights's ongoing efforts to hold Donald Rumsfeld accountable for the war crimes he has committed in Iraq and at Guantánamo. While the two cases filed in Germany have both been dismissed by the German federal prosecutor and are on appeal, we have recently filed in France, and are continuing our fight to hold Rumsfeld and all the other officials who justified and promoted torture and abuse accountable for their crimes.

A Brief History of the Center for Constitutional Rights

For more than forty years, the Center for Constitutional Rights has fought to protect and advance the rights of those on the margins and to challenge the powers that be. We were birthed in the midst of the civil rights struggle in the 1960s by four activist attorneys who saw that peoples' movements needed legal support. Today, we continue to challenge overreaching executive authority, fight repression and attacks on political dissent, and defend the rights of people of color to be free of police brutality and racial profiling.

Our history is not only filled with groundbreaking legal victories, but also important moral victories—times when we may have lost in the courts but won in the court of public opinion. We defended the Chicago Eight from charges of conspiracy, fought for Fannie Lou Hamer's right to vote in Mississippi, and brought the first case that defended a woman's right to an abortion, rather than a doctor's right to practice. In the 1970s, we pioneered the use of a little-known U.S. statute—known as the Alien Tort Statute—as a tool to hold human rights violators from around the world accountable for their crimes in U.S. courts, no matter where they are from.

Today's challenges are no less complex than those of the past, and we have met them with the same sort of determined resistance that we did in the previous decades.

Post-9/11, we have fought the PATRIOT Act, the government practice of extraordinary rendition, material support statutes that criminalize lawful First Amendment activities, and illegal government spying of Americans, and defended the rights of Muslim, Arab, and South Asian men who were racially profiled and rounded up after 9/11 and held by the U.S. government. We have brought cases against private contractors working in Iraq, including Blackwater Worldwide, to hold them accountable for the murders of dozens of innocent Iraqi bystanders.

And we were the first organization to defend the rights of the men held at Guantánamo Bay. In that hyper-patriotic atmosphere immediately after the attacks, no one else wanted to go near these men, fearing the taint of "terrorism." People believed, as Vice President Dick Cheney claimed, that these men were the "worst of the worst."

The Center for Constitutional Rights has never shied away from controversial cases, and we believe that the past six years have shown that we took the principled and ethical stand when we said that these men held in prison by the U.S. government possess basic human rights that must not be violated.

When the torture of the men at Guantánamo and subsequently the torture of Iraqi prisoners at Abu Ghraib came to light, more people and organizations began demanding that the U.S. government be held accountable for its crimes.

CCR went one step further: we actually took Secretary of State Donald Rumsfeld and other high-ranking government officials to court in Germany and France, charging them with war crimes, crimes against humanity, and torture for their role in the abuse of men, women, and children at Guantánamo Bay and at Abu Ghraib. In 2004 and then in 2006, we filed two separate complaints in Germany, both of which were dismissed by the German federal prosecutor for political reasons. In 2007 we filed a third complaint in France. We are continuing to use the courts in our attempt to bring justice to the victims of the torture authorized and promoted by Rumsfeld and other high-ranking officials in the Bush administration.

This book is yet another way we are holding Rumsfeld and other U.S. government officials accountable for the program of torture they instituted and authorized post-9/11. This is our case against torture and against Donald Rumsfeld.

Vincent Warren
Executive Director
Center for Constitutional Rights

From Pinochet to Rumsfeld

> The Pinochet litigation marks a milestone in the evolu-
> tion of international law. It confirms that, at least in
> respect of public officials other than a serving head of
> state, the doctrine of state or sovereign immunity is no
> bar to the exercise of universal jurisdiction over such
> officials.
>
> —Sir Nigel Rodley, former U.N. Special
> Representative for Torture[1]

Given the linear path from the Pinochet case in the United
Kingdom to the Rumsfeld case in Germany, it may be useful to
examine how the one has led to the other. Let us begin with a
look at what these two paragons of modern-day torture have in
common.

Both come from middle-class beginnings that would give no
indication of their future as human rights abusers. From those
beginnings, both men arrived at positions of considerable power
at a relatively young age, on their way to the pinnacle of power in
their respective countries. Neither Rumsfeld nor Pinochet could
have been characterized as rabid right-wingers until the late
stages of their careers. Rumsfeld was intensely interested and
active in politics, but was at first regarded more as a technocrat and
administrator than a member or leader of the ultra-conservative
wing of the Republican Party. Similarly, the pre-coup Pinochet dis-
played no particular traits of character or mindset that would have
led one to predict that he would wind up as one of the great mass
murderers of the twentieth century. After Allende's ascension to
power he was a loyal supporter of the socialist regime in the
nonpolitical tradition of the Chilean army. He was the last of the
military officers to join the conspiracy to overthrow the Allende
regime before throwing himself wholeheartedly into the task of
erasing every vestige thereof.

Paranoia and Megalomania

From the moment they became supreme commanders of their respective operations—Rumsfeld's against "terrorism" and Pinochet's against "Marxism"—both men saw themselves as generals in a war to save civilization, to be fought with no holds barred. For Rumsfeld the moment came on September 11, 2001; for Pinochet it had come on the same date twenty-eight years earlier. Both saw themselves invested with a divine or at least historical mission to defeat "these really bad people," as Rumsfeld characterized the hundreds of hapless Guantánamo detainees in one of his congressional appearances. Neither seems to have known much about who "these people" really were. Pinochet couldn't tell the difference between a communist, a socialist, and a social democrat; Rumsfeld came to the "war on terror" with a fatally flawed vision of the complexities of facts on the ground, inherited from his neoconservative friends.

Faux Legalism

Although both Rumsfeld and Pinochet carried out their self-appointed missions with no holds barred and no regard for constitutional principles or moral values, each found it necessary to cover his conduct with the appearance of legality. In Pinochet's case, this took the form of an endless stream of decree-laws which he promulgated after dissolving the democratically elected parliament. Rumsfeld, along with Cheney and Bush, found a covey of compliant lawyers in the Pentagon and the Department of Justice to furnish them with legal opinions justifying their every illegal action, including the invasion of Iraq and the indefinite detention and torture of vast numbers of "unlawful enemy combatants."

The Pinochet Litigation

On that fateful day in 1973 when Pinochet's thugs stormed the Moneda, the presidential palace in Chile, Salvador Allende asked his political advisor Juan Garces to leave the palace and tell the world what had happened.

Garces carried out this mission in a number of books and articles, but he did more than that: in 1996, using a little-known provision of Spanish law, he, along with the Association of Progressive Prosecutors of Spain, filed a complaint against Pinochet and a number of other high officials of his regime for genocide, terrorism, torture, forced disappearance, illegal detention, and murder. Under the law of Spain and many other "code countries"—as opposed to common law countries like the United States—such complaints, if valid factually, would result in official indictments prosecuted by the state.[2]

Because Spanish law does not provide for trials *in absentia*, the case could not go forward until Pinochet made the mistake of showing up in London in September 1998 for back surgery and to renew contact with his friend Margaret Thatcher. On October 15, the Spanish judge to whom the Pinochet case had been assigned and who had made a name for himself in the vigorous prosecution of terrorism cases, was tipped off to the fact that Pinochet was about to return to Chile. He immediately issued to the British authorities a request for Pinochet's arrest with a view to his extradition to Spain. Upon being advised by the Foreign Office that Pinochet did not enjoy diplomatic immunity, a magistrate, contacted at his home by the metropolitan police, issued a warrant for his arrest, which was promptly carried out in Pinochet's hospital room.

From that point on, "the Pinochet affair" was headline material throughout the world. It was not only avidly followed by legal specialists but also by human rights activists and the thousands of Pinochet's victims and their survivors. There was also a sense in the public at large that something of enormous consequence was occurring, a turning of the tide of impunity, a demonstration that no matter how high the mighty rose they could be brought down to the bar of justice.

But of course it was not to be that simple. Pinochet's lawyers won the first move, persuading the High Court of Justice for England and Wales to vacate the arrest warrant on the ground that their client was entitled to immunity as a former head of state and that the offenses with which he was charged were not extraditable offenses because immunity remained.

Eventually, the House of Lords found that Pinochet did not have immunity from arrest and extradition, but they did so for a bewildering array of sometimes conflicting reasons. The majority did not adopt the holding that he possessed immunity because the crimes were committed in his official capacity; only two of the Lords did so.[3] Rather, the analysis focused on the Convention Against Torture, which all three countries—Chile, Spain, and the United Kingdom—had ratified and implemented in their domestic legislation and which defined torture as an international crime; i.e., one that could be no part of "public policy."

But this, as is well known, was not the end of the matter. Amenability to torture was one thing; actual extradition was another, to be decided by the U.K.'s Home Secretary, Jack Straw. Originally he had ordered the extradition to proceed; eventually, following the submission of papers concerning Pinochet's medical condition by his lawyers, as well as a medical report commissioned by the Secretary himself, Straw decided that Pinochet's mental state was such that he could not receive a fair trial anywhere and therefore should not be extradited. The much criticized decision bore all the earmarks of a political deal between the president of Chile, the prime minister of the United Kingdom, and the prime minister of Spain.

Pinochet promptly returned to Chile. He died of a stroke on December 10, 2006, under house arrest and disgraced even in the eyes of many of his former supporters.

While he thus escaped the trial and punishment he so richly deserved, the nearly successful efforts to bring him to justice have helped to move the struggle against the impunity of the high and mighty a giant step forward. The shadow of the Pinochet case hovered over the deliberations that led to the creation of the International Criminal Court in 2002, as well as the universal jurisdiction law unanimously adopted by the German parliament in the same year.[4]

The 1998 decision of the U.K. High Court that genocide and crimes against humanity are not extraditable offenses if performed by heads of state in their official capacity may well be the last such decision in the annals of law. The creativity of the lawyers who maintained their determination to bring Pinochet to justice and of the victims, human rights activists, and outraged citizens who spurred them on will serve as an inspiring example to those who say "no" to torture, mass murder, forced disappearance, and other methods of "public policy" that have no place in a decent world.

Peter Weiss
Vice President
Center for Constitutional Rights

Establishing Responsibility for Human Rights Violations—The Role of Universal Criminal Jurisdiction

This section outlines the current state of universal jurisdiction practice over serious crimes under international criminal law—genocide, crimes against humanity, war crimes, and torture—and reflects on lessons learned in the increasing number of universal jurisdiction cases before national courts over recent years. The recourse of a rising number of countries to universal jurisdiction to ensure accountability for the worst human rights violations underlines that the principle has become a reality in the fight against impunity.

The concept of universal jurisdiction is no longer confined to legal theory.* The principle of universal jurisdiction allows the national authorities of any state to investigate and, where there is sufficient evidence, prosecute persons for serious international crimes committed outside a state's territory—including those with no particular connection to that state. This principle is based on the notion that some crimes—such as genocide, crimes against humanity, war crimes, and torture—are of such exceptional gravity that they affect the fundamental interests of the international community as a whole.

Universal jurisdiction confers on a state the competence to prosecute a perpetrator regardless of the location of the crime and the nationality of the victim or the perpetrator. The only condition for an exercise of universal jurisdiction is therefore not—as in traditional doctrines of jurisdiction—nationality, location, or national interests, but rather the nature of the crime.

The concept of universal jurisdiction today applies to a wide range of crimes and is provided for in international treaties, such as the Geneva Conventions and the Convention Against Torture, as well as customary law. Recent years have seen a rising number

---

*The views and opinions expressed are those are those of the authors and do not necessarily reflect those of REDRESS and FIDH.

of universal jurisdiction cases filed before national courts in Europe, North America, and, only very recently, Latin America and Africa. After a long period of neglect, the reason for states to apply universal jurisdiction can be attributed to a rising interest of the international community in holding accountable those responsible for the worst crimes: genocide, crimes against humanity, war crimes, and torture. The development was kicked off with the establishment of the ad-hoc tribunals for the former Yugoslavia and Rwanda in 1993 and 1994 respectively, and extended to the establishment of the internationalized courts such as the Special Court for Sierra Leone and the Extraordinary Chambers in the Courts for Cambodia. The efforts to ensure individual criminal accountability culminated in the creation of the International Criminal Court on July 1, 2002.

Originally applied to hold pirates and slave traders accountable, the principle of universal jurisdiction today extends to terrorists and human-rights offending former heads of state alike.[5] The International Military Tribunal (IMT) at Nuremberg extended the principle to include war crimes and crimes against humanity, and universal jurisdiction was key for establishing accountability in several post-WWII trials following the IMT.[6] The obligation of state parties to seek out and prosecute those said to be responsible for grave breaches of international humanitarian law is a key aspect of the four Geneva Conventions of 1949.[7] Grave breaches include willful killing, torture, or inhuman treatment, including biological experiments and willfully causing great suffering or serious injury to body or health.[8] Treaties such as the United Nations Convention against Torture and Cruel, Inhuman, and Degrading Treatment or Punishment[9] and the Convention on the Protection of all Persons from Enforced Disappearances[10] include the obligation to prosecute or extradite accused persons found on the territory of parties to the Convention, irrespective of where the crimes were committed.

International customary law permits states to exercise universal jurisdiction over genocide crimes against humanity and war crimes that are not grave breaches of the Geneva Conventions.[11] The "modern" doctrine of universal jurisdiction therefore covers serious crimes under international law.

While the courts of the state in which the crime took place (the territorial state) would appear to be the preferred jurisdiction to afford justice to victims, there are several reasons for establishing universal jurisdiction over "grave-breach" crimes. One benefit is that it provides victims of international crimes access to justice, especially in cases where the crimes were state-sponsored and the state is reluctant to prosecute the criminal, or in instances where the judicial system of the state has been destroyed by civil war or strife.

Universal jurisdiction proceedings can further serve as an important catalyst for judicial action in the territorial state. The arrest of former Chilean dictator Augusto Pinochet in October 1998 in London, for instance, inspired victims in Chile to initiate proceedings before Chilean courts. The victims had previously kept silent, until the filing of the complaint in European countries.

As a reserve tool to justice, universal jurisdiction can play a crucial role in securing evidence of serious international crimes, which can be vital for future proceedings, either in the territorial state or, on the basis of universal jurisdiction, in another third state. Even in respect to countries whose current governments are reluctant to prosecute, governments change over time and future leaders may be willing to bring those responsible for past violations of human rights to justice before their own courts. In such circumstances, evidence taken in third countries (on the basis of universal jurisdiction) in the immediate aftermath of the crimes is crucial, in particular with respect to testimony of witnesses able to escape to such third countries.

There are some necessary requirements for an effective exercise of universal jurisdiction. These include first and foremost political will as well as dedicated individuals. An international framework providing for cooperation and exchange, that guarantees effective and efficient investigation and prosecution, is equally important. While the number of states applying the principle in practice is increasing, it remains low. To be truly universal, the exercise of universal jurisdiction will need to expand to countries outside of the European Union or North America. Experiences need to be shared more widely, and national authorities must be trained to ensure effective investigations. The true *raison d'être* of universal jurisdiction as well as its legal basis needs to be communicated to all sectors of civil society and to governments, in order to counter claims that universal jurisdiction is a political tool. And finally, countries that are in the process of applying universal jurisdiction in practice but lack the financial and personal resources to do so, need the support of the international community.

Juergen Schurr
Project Coordinator, "Universal Jurisdiction"
REDRESS

Jeanne Sulzer
Legal Action Group
International Federation for Human Rights (FIDH)

CCR's 2004 and 2006 German War Crimes Cases Against Donald Rumsfeld and Others

By the summer of 2004, it was clear that, in the United States at least, there would be no legal consequences for the criminally responsible superiors who allowed the abuse at Guantánamo and Abu Ghraib to occur.

Despite the many governmental and investigational reports documenting human rights violations at Abu Ghraib, the Bush administration's "rotten apple theory" that the abuses and torture were the exclusive responsibility of rogue lower-level military personnel was gaining currency in the media and the public.

As a result, the Center for Constitutional Rights in 2004 decided to make use of the criminal universal jurisdiction tool not only to make a case against Rumsfeld, but to make the case against torture. We chose Germany because it has the best law on universal jurisdiction, and because some of the Abu Ghraib torturers were stationed at U.S. military bases in Germany.

In tandem with the founding of the International Criminal Court (ICC) in 2002, the German Parliament had approved by wide margins the Code of Crimes against International Law (CCIL), making it one of the first domestic legislative bodies in the world to regulate international criminal law after the creation of the ICC. The objective of the German Code was "to better define crimes against international law than is currently possible under general criminal law" and "to make it absolutely clear that Germany is always in a position to prosecute for itself those crimes falling under the jurisdiction of the ICC Statute."[12] In the first paragraph of the German Code, the principle of universal jurisdiction is specifically prescribed for those crimes against international law defined in the Code, "even where the act was committed abroad and has no correlation to the home country."

The 2004 Rumsfeld Case

On November 29, 2004, CCR filed the first criminal complaint against Rumsfeld and other high-ranking officials with the German Federal Prosecutor's Office at the Karlsruhe Court. The four Iraqi plaintiffs in the case were victims of gruesome crimes while at Abu Ghraib, including torture by means of severe and repeated beatings; sleep, food, and clothing deprivation; forced nakedness; hooding; and sexual abuse. The U.S. officials charged were accused of having committed war crimes against detainees in Iraq, Afghanistan, and at Guantánamo.

In this case, there were particularly compelling reasons for the German Federal Prosecutor—the German official in charge of investigating such complaints—to exercise his duty to prosecute. First of all, the grave nature of the crimes coupled with extensive evidence of officials' direct involvement demanded an investigation. Second, the United States, which had primary jurisdiction to prosecute the authors of the crimes, was in no way willing to look up the chain of command, thereby justifying Germany's use of secondary jurisdiction. Third, three of the defendants were stationed in Germany at the time CCR filed the case. Others, such as Rumsfeld, often traveled to Germany, and the military units that had engaged in the illegal conduct in Iraq were now stationed in Germany. Although such links to Germany are unnecessary for the prosecutor to fulfill his or her duty, when the alleged perpetrators are actually on German soil, the duty to investigate is even stronger. Lastly, the fact that the complainants were the direct victims of the abuses placed an additional duty on the prosecutor to respond to their call for justice.

Not surprisingly, as soon as the lawsuit against Donald Rumsfeld was made public, the Pentagon, in various press conferences, warned German authorities that such "frivolous lawsuits," if taken seriously by the German judiciary, would affect the broader relationship between the two countries. By the end of January 2005, as the German Federal Prosecutor still had not officially refused to begin investigating the allegations made in the complaint, the U.S. embassy in Germany announced that Secretary of State Rumsfeld had canceled a previously scheduled trip to Munich for the Munich Security Conference.

On February 10, 2005, a day before the opening of the Munich Security Conference, the Federal Prosecutor's Office issued a decision not to open an investigation into the case, enabling Rumsfeld to visit Munich, which he did two days later. The decision was justified on the grounds that German investigative authorities would not take action unless and until the United States formally declined to prosecute. "There are no indications that the authorities and courts of the United States of America are refraining, or would refrain, from penal measures as regards the violations described in the complaint."[13]

Subsequent petitions to the German Prosecutor for reconsideration and an appeal were dismissed, leaving the German case against Rumsfeld, at least for the time being, at a dead end. CCR could not itself file a case in the United States, as criminal cases can be initiated only by federal prosecutors.

Eighteen months later, the United States passed the Military Commissions Act on October 17, 2006, purporting to give amnesty to U.S. officials. This, along with the fact that all interim investigations in the United States were directed toward the criminal culpability of only the lowest-ranking military personnel, seemed to contradict the German court's finding in 2005 that there were "no indications" that the U.S. authorities and courts "would refrain from penal measures" regarding the allegations.

In November 2006, three organizations—the CCR, the FIDH, and the Republican Attorney's Association (RAV)—filed an updated four-hundred-page complaint with the German Prosecutor on behalf of twelve Iraqi citizens who had been abused in Abu Ghraib and one Saudi citizen—Mohammed al Qahtani—still held at Guantánamo. The new complaint received support from dozens of international human rights groups and leading figures from various regions in the world. Nobel Peace Prize winner Aldolfo Perez Esquirel, alternative Nobel Peace Prize winner Martín Almada, and Theo van Boven, the former United Nations Special Rapporteur on Torture, signed on as co-plaintiffs.

In this second version of the complaint, fourteen high-ranking officials were named as defendants.[14] Importantly, Rumsfeld's resignation the week before the filing meant that he could no longer claim immunity as a government official. Former White House Counsel (and then-Attorney General) Alberto Gonzales, former Deputy Attorney General John Yoo, and former Assistant Attorney General Jay Bybee, as well as others, were named and alleged to be the legal architects of the Bush administration's practice of torture.

The existence of their legal memos and the authorizations by Rumsfeld, LTG Sanchez, and others of special interrogation techniques that violate humanitarian and human rights law-made it clear that responsibility for abusive treatment at Abu Ghraib and other U.S. facilities extends all the way to the top tiers of the U.S. government. President Bush and Vice President Dick Cheney, as the head of state and the successor head of state, respectively, possess immunity from criminal indictment while they are in office for acts that occurred during their tenure. The moment their terms are over, they can join the others as defendants.

But, once again, the German government declined to prosecute. On April 27, 2007, Germany's new Federal Prosecutor announced that she would not proceed with an investigation, despite the fact that the German code expressly states Germany's universal duty to fight torture and other serious crimes. Federal Prosecutor Monika Harms cited as grounds for dismissal the facts that the crimes were committed outside of Germany, and the defendants neither resided in Germany, were currently located in Germany, nor would they soon enter German territory. (Actually, we believed some of the defendants were still residing in Germany, but without the Prosecutor's help, it could not be proven; in 2005, when three of the defendants *were* still living in Germany, the complainants' argument that a domestic link was present was not recognized in any way by the Prosecutor or the Court of Appeal.)

The prosecutor also stated that investigations would not have a reasonable chance of succeeding. No reference was made to the large number of available documents and governmental memos, or to the fact that attorneys in the case had secured the cooperation of General Janis Karpinski, former commander of Abu Ghraib and other U.S.-run prisons in Iraq, as well as other witnesses and victims. Janis Karpinski and others had confirmed in the complaint that they were willing to travel to Germany, to testify before the court or to any German embassy, or simply to meet with the prosecutors to help them determine how best to proceed with the case. These witnesses were never called upon. This decision was appealed in November 2007, and a response to the appeal is still pending.

"Success Without Victory" or Just Another Defeat?

To date, Germany has failed to play its stated role of holding torturers accountable. While future administrations of the United States will ultimately need to examine the criminal responsibility of its current and former high-ranking officials, it is absolutely fundamental for foreign courts to begin investigating the allegations now. To date, none of the plaintiffs—and the hundreds of other detainees subjected to similar abuses—has seen justice, and none of those who authorized these techniques at the top of the chain of command has been held liable or investigated by an independent body.

History has shown that, ultimately, universal jurisdiction investigations can lead to unexpected legal successes, as in the case of Augusto Pinochet. Meanwhile the criminal complaints filed in Germany, aimed at holding powerful officials accountable, initiated legal discussions within and outside the legal community and, in 2006, a worldwide discussion on Rumsfeld's involvement in the U.S. torture program. Perhaps these will ultimately be seen in retrospect as the first critical steps in a ground-breaking enforcement of universal human rights.

Wolfgang Kaleck
ECCHR

Claire Tixeire
FIDH-CCR

Complete List of Organizations and Co-Plaintiffs Involved

Unprecedented Support for the Case

When a complaint is filed to the Federal Prosecutor, any group or individual may join the complaint as a "co-plaintiff," which demonstrates the support of these groups or individuals and their common request for the opening of an investigation. Co-plaintiffs in the present case include:

Individuals

> 1980 Nobel Peace Prize winner Aldolfo Perez Esquirel (Argentina)
>
> 2002 Nobel Peace Prize winner Martín Almada (Paraguay)
>
> Theo van Boven, former United Nations Special Rapporteur on Torture
>
> Sister Dianna Ortiz, torture survivor, Executive Director of Torture Abolition and Survivors Support Coalition International (TAASC)

International and Regional NGOs

> FIDH: International Federation for Human Rights
>
> The International Peace Bureau (Nobel Peace Prize winner in 1910)
>
> International Association of Lawyers Against Nuclear Arms (IALANA)
>
> European Democratic Lawyers
>
> European Democratic Jurists
>
> International Association of Democratic Lawyers

National NGOs

> Argentina: Comité de Acción Jurídica (CAJ)
>
> Argentina: Liga Argentina por los Derechos del Hombre

Bahrain: Bahrain Human Rights Society (BHRS)

Canada: Lawyers against the War (LAW)

Chile: Asociación Americana de Juristas, Section Chile

Colombia: Colectivo de Abogados José Alvear Restrepo

Democratic Republic of Congo: Association Africaine des Droits de l'Homme (ASADHO)

Ecuador: Fundación Regional de Asesoría en Derechos Humanos (INREDH)

Egypt: Egyptian Organization for Human Rights (EOHR)

El Salvador: Comisión de Derechos Humanos de El Salvador (CDHES)

France: Ligue Française des Droits de l'Homme (LDH)

France: Association pour la défense du droit international humanitaire (ADIF)

France: Droit- Solidarité

Germany: The Republican Attorneys' Association (RAV)

Germany: Medizinische Flüchtlingshilf

Guatemala: Comisión de Derechos Humanos de Guatemala (CDHG)

Italy: Giuristi Democratici

Italy: Unione Forense per la Tutela dei Diritti dell'Uomo

Jordan: Amman Center for Human Rights Studies (ACHR)

Mexico: Comisión Mexicana de Defensa y Promoción de los Derechos Humanos (CMDPDH)

Mexico: Liga Mexicana por la Defensa de los Derechos Humanos (LIMEDDH)

Nicaragua: Centro Nicaraguense de Derechos Humanos (CENIDH)

Palestine: Palestinian Center for Human Rights

Panama: Centro de Capacitación Social (CCS)

Peru: Asociacion Pro Derechos Humanos (APRODEH)

Peru: Asesoría Laboral del Perú

Senegal: Rencontre Africaine pour la Défense des Droits de l'Homme (RADDHO)

Spain: Asociación Catalana per al Defensa de Drets Humans (ACDDH)

Spain: Asociación Libre de Abogados (ALA)

Tchad: Association Tchadienne pour la Promotion et la Défense des Droits de l'Homme (ATPDH)

Tunisia: Ligue Tunisienne des Droits de l'Homme (LTDH)

USA: The Center for Constitutional Rights (CCR)

USA: National Lawyers' Guild (NLG)

USA: Torture Abolition and Survivors Support Coalition International (TASSC)

USA: Veterans for Peace

Notes

1. Opening Statement

1. Aliya Mughal, "The Only Thing that Torture Guarantees is Pain; It Never Guarantees the Truth," December 11, 2006, Medical Foundation for the Care of Victims of Torture, available at www.torturecare.org.uk/news/features/818.

2. See Brad Garrett's story, available at www.washingtonian.com/articles/people/4700.html.

3. Reuters, "Geneva Convention Doesn't Cover Detainees," January 11, 2002, available at www.crimelynx.com/nogen.html.

2. Summary of the Indictment

1. The four Geneva Conventions of 1949, ratified by the United States in 1955, protect all individuals from torture or inhuman treatment in war time—detainees must at all times be humanely treated (Geneva III, arts. 13, 17, & 87; Geneva IV, arts. 27 & 32)—they must not be subjected to any form of "physical or mental coercion" (Geneva III, art. 17; Geneva IV, arts. 27 & 31).

Torture or inhuman treatment of prisoners of war or protected persons are grave breaches of the Geneva Conventions, and are considered war crimes (Geneva III, art. 130; Geneva IV, art. 147). Common Article 3 to the Geneva Conventions also prohibits "[v]iolence to life and person, in particular murder of all kinds, mutilation, cruel treatment and torture; . . . outrages upon personal dignity, in particular humiliating and degrading treatment." Even persons who are not entitled to the protections of the 1949 Geneva Conventions are protected by the "fundamental guarantees" of art. 75 of Protocol I of 1977 to the Geneva Conventions. The War Crimes Act of 1996 (18 U.S.C. § 2441) makes it a criminal offense for U.S. military personnel and U.S. nationals to commit war crimes as specified in the 1949 Geneva Conventions.

2. President George W. Bush Military Order, November 13, 2001.

3. Jason Vest, "Implausible Denial II," *The Nation*, May 17, 2004.

4. Seymour Hersh, "Blank," *The New Yorker*, May 24, 2004.

5. Associated Press, "MPs Were Urged to 'Soften Up' Prisoners, Report Says," May 8, 2004.

6. "Fear up" is one of the harsh interrogation methods authorized by Donald Rumsfeld, as detailed in the Schlesinger Report.

7. See, for example, Jane Mayer, "The Memo," *The New Yorker*, February 27, 2006.

8. Jane Mayer, "The Hidden Power," *The New Yorker*, July 3, 2006.

3. Evidence for the Prosecution

1. Letter re: Suspected Mistreatment of Detainees, from T.J. Harrington, Deputy Assistant Director, Counterterrorism Division, FBI, to Major General Donald R. Ryder, Criminal Investigation Command, Department of the Army, July 14, 2006.

2. According to several reports, Mr. al Qahtani was held in isolation for 160 days, during which time he was subjected to a variety of other interrogation methods, including twenty-hour long interrogations combined with severe sleep deprivation. See Schmidt Report at 20.

3. Interrogation Log 01/02/2003 at 0100.

4. See PHR Report at 5.

5. It is unclear how often this occurred. The log documents it explicitly twice: 12/03/2002 at 2105: "Detainee's head and beard were shaved with electric clippers. Detainee started resistance when beard was shaved and MPs had to restrain. Shaving was halted until detainee was once more compliant. LTC P supervised shaving. No problems occurred. Photos were taken of detainee when the shaving was finished"; 12/18/2002 at 1415: "Detainee's head and beard were shaved with electric clippers. Detainee started to struggle when the beard was touched but quickly became compliant"; 12/20/2002 at 2020: "Lt G entered the interrogation booth and gave detainee an even shave. The detainee did not resist"; 01/11/2003 at 0230: "Source received haircut. Detainee did not resist until the beard was cut. Detainee stated he would talk about anything if his beard was left alone. Interrogator asked detainee if he would be honest about himself. Detainee replied "if God wills." Beard was shaven."

Military authorities have forcibly shaved Mr. al Qahtani in violation of his religious beliefs and practices as recently as the end of 2005, prior to his first meeting with his attorney.

6. 12/12/2002 at 0001: "Upon entering the booth, lead played the call to prayer with a special alarm clock. Detainee was told, 'this is no longer the call to prayer. You're not allowed to pray. This is the call to interrogation. So pay attention.'"

7. Numerous instances are recorded. For example: 11/28/2002 at 0630: "When control entered booth, detainee stated in English 'Excuse me sergeant, I want to pray.' Control said 'Have you earned prayer? I know you have a lot to ask forgiveness for, but I already told you that you have to earn it.' Detainee says 'Please, I want to pray here' (pointing to floor next to his chair). Control responds no"; 12/06/2002 at 1600: "Detainee allowed to pray after promising to continue cooperating"; 12/14/2002 at 0001: "Detainee's hands were cuffed at his sides to prevent him from conducting his prayer ritual."

8. (1) 12/04/2002 at 1800: "The detainee was bothered by the presence and touch of a female"; (2) 12/05/2002 at 1800: "Detainee became irritated with the female invading his personal space"; (3) 12/06/2002 at 1930: "The approaches employed [included] Invasion of Space by a Female"; (4) 12/09/2002 at 2340: "Detainee was repulsed by the female invasion of his personal space"; (5) 12/10/2002 at 1830: "Detainee became very annoyed with the female invading his personal space"; (6a) 12/12/2002 at 1830: "SGT L started 'invasion of personal space' approach"; (6b) 12/12/2002 at 2312: "The detainee is still annoyed with the female invasion of space"; (7) 12/19/2002 at 2320: "He attempts to resist female contact"; (8) 12/21/2002 at 2223: "He was laid out on the floor so I straddled him without putting my weight on him"; (9) 12/23/2002 at 2245: "Female interrogator used invasion of personal space and detainee cried out to Allah several times"; (10) 12/25/2002 at 1929: "Detainee spoke in English when the female interrogator invaded his personal space."

9. See, e.g., 12/20/2002 at 2200: "The detainee was stripped searched. Initially he was attempting to resist the guards. After approximately five minutes of nudity the detainee ceased to resist. He would only stare at the wall with GREAT focus. His eyes were squinted and stuck on one point on the wall directly in front of him. He later stated that he knew there was nothing he could do with so many guards around him, so why should he resist. He stated that he did not like the females viewing his naked body while being searched and felt if he could have done something about it then he would have."

10. 12/12/2003 at 1115: "In order to escalate the detainee's emotions, a mask was made from an MRE box with a smiley face on it and placed on the detainee's head for a few moments. A latex glove was inflated and

labeled the "sissy slap" glove. This glove was touched to the detainee's face periodically after explaining the terminology to him. The mask was placed back on the detainee's head. While wearing the mask, the team began dance instruction with the detainee. The detainee became agitated and began shouting."

11. 12/20/2002 at 1300: "A towel was placed on the detainee's head like a burka with his face exposed and the interrogator proceeded to give the detainee dance lessons. The detainee became agitated and tried to kick an MP. No retaliation was used for the kick and the dance lesson continued."

12. 12/17/2002 at 2100: "Detainee appeared to have been disturbed by the word homosexual. He did not appear to appreciate being called a homosexual. He denies being a homosexual. He also appeared to be very annoyed by the use of his mother and sister as examples of prostitutes and whores."

13. (1) 12/19/2002 at 0200: "While walking out, detainee pulled a picture of a model off (it had been fashioned into a sign to hang around his neck)"; (2) 12/23/2002 at 0001: "Upon entering booth, lead changed white noise music and hung pictures of swimsuit models around his neck. Detainee was left in booth listening to white noise"; (3) 12/24/2002 at 0001: "Control entered booth, changed music playing, and hung binder of fitness models around detainee's neck"; (4) 12/26/2002 at 0001: "Detainee was eating his food (given by the previous team). Lead walked into booth turned on white noise and put picture binder of swimsuit models over detainees neck."

14. (1) 12/17/2002 at 2200: "He appeared disgusted by the photos of UBL and a variety of sexy females. Detainee would avoid looking at all of the photos shown to him"; (2) 12/19/2002 at 0300: "Interrogators had detainee look at pictures of women in bikinis and identify if the women were the same or different. Detainee refused to look at girls and began struggling. A few drops of water were sprinkled on his head to gain compliance"; (3) 12/20/2002 at 0001: "Detainee listened to white noise while interrogators added photos of fitness models to a binder. Once completed, the interrogators began showing the photos and asking the detainee detailed questions about the photos"; (4) 12/21/2002 at 0001: "New interrogation shift enters the booth and begins "attention to detail" approach. Detainee looks at photos of fitness models and answers questions about the photos"; (5) 12/22/2002 at 0030: "Lead began the "attention to detail" theme with the fitness model photos. Detainee refused to look at photos claiming it was against his religion. Lead poured a 24 oz bottle of water over detainee's head. Detainee then began to look at photos"; (6) 12/23/2002: "The 'attention to detail' approach began. Lead pulled pictures of swimsuit models off detainee and told him the test of his ability to answer questions

would begin. Detainee refused to answer and finally stated that he would after lead poured water over detainees head and was told he would be subjected to this treatment day after day"; (7) 12/24/2002 at 0200: "Control entered the booth and began the "attention to detail" lesson for the night. The detainee still would not accurately answer questions about the fitness models and control stated that the lesson would continue the next day"; (8) 12/26/2002 at 0030: "Lead entered the booth and began attention to detail approach. Detainee missed 3 of 10 questions. He has learned to provide more details and provides enough information to substantiate his answers"; (9) 12/27/2002 at 0100: "Detainee was taken to bathroom and walked 10 minutes. The "attention to detail" theme was run with the fitness model photos."

15. 11/25/2002 at 1000: "Detainee again said he has to go to bathroom. SGT R said he can go in the bottle. Detainee said he wanted to go to the bathroom because it's more comfortable. SGT R said 'You've ruined all trust, you can either go in the bottle or in your pants.' Detainee goes in his pants."

16. 12/21/2002 at 1630: "Detainee given shower, brushed teeth, and given new uniform. The detainee was very shy and asked several times to cover himself with his trousers or a towel while in the shower."

17. Schmidt Report. This is documented in the interrogation log as follows: 12/20/2002 at 1115, 1300: "Told detainee that a dog is held in higher esteem because dogs know right from wrong and know to protect innocent people from bad people. Began teaching the detainee lessons such as stay, come, and bark to elevate his social status up to that of a dog. Detainee became very agitated." Then: "Dog tricks continued and detainee stated he should be treated like a man. Detainee was told he would have to learn who to defend and who to attack. Interrogator showed photos of 9-11 victims and told detainee he should bark happy for these people. Interrogator also showed photos of Al Qaida terrorists and told detainee he should growl at these people."

18. Neil A. Lewis, "Fresh Details Emerge on Harsh Methods at Guantánamo," *New York Times*, January 1, 2005.

19. Report of the International Committee of the Red Cross (ICRC) on the Treatment by the Coalition Forces of Prisoners of War and Other Protected Persons by the Geneva Conventions in Iraq During Arrest, Internment, and Interrogation, February 2004.

20. See Taguba Report.

21. See Taguba Report, p. 16

22. As advanced by Seymour Hersh, in a July 2004 ACLU Members Conference "America at a Crossroads," and in his book *Chain of Command: The Road from 9/11 to Abu Ghraib* (New York: HarperPerennial, 2005).

23. See BBC News, "Top General Heads Iraq Jail Probe," June 17, 2004, available at http://news.bbc.co.uk/2/hi/americas/3815311.stm.

24. See Schlesinger Report, p. 5.

25. Emily Bazelon, "From Bagram to Abu Ghraib," *Mother Jones*, March/April 2005, available at www.motherjones.com/news/feature/2005/03/03_2005_Bazelon.html.

26. *Ibid.*

27. Abu Ghraib is also referred to as the Baghdad Central Correctional Facility, or BCCF.

28. See the June 12, 2002, memo from U.S. Attorney Paul J. McNulty that states that "the Secretary of Defense's counsel [William Haynes] had authorized him to 'take the gloves off'" in interrogating John Walker Lindh.

29. Kai Ambos, *Commentary on the Rome Statute of the International Criminal Court: Observers' Notes, Article by Article*, ed. Otto Triffterer (Baden Baden: Nomos, 1999), p. 480.

30. Scott Horton, "January 2005 Affidavit," submitted as part of the 2004 German complaint against Donald Rumsfeld.

31. The case involved Aidan Delgado; see David DeBatto, "Whitewashing Torture?" *Salon*, December 8, 2004. Available at http://dir.salon.com/story/news/feature/2004/12/08/coverup/index.html.

32. See Human Rights Watch, "By the Numbers: Findings of the Detainee Abuse and Accountability Project," April 2006, available at http://hrw.org/reports/2006/ct0406/3.htm.

33. *Ibid.*

34. Brig. Gen. (Ret.) John H. Johns, "Torture and National Security," May 9, 2005, available at www.armscontrolcenter.org/archives/001586.php.

35. However, as we explain in earlier pages, while even the Bush administration said Geneva Conventions were to be fully applied in Iraq, in reality techniques were used that fell far outside what is permissible under the Conventions.

36. JIDC stands for Joint Interrogation and Debriefing Center.

4. Witnesses and Statements for the Defense

1. Reuters, "Geneva Convention Doesn't Cover Detainees," January 11, 2002, available at www.crimelynx.com/nogen.html.

2. Jim Garamone, "Joint Strike Fighter Signing Ceremony," DefenseLink News (US Military), American Forces Press Service, February 7, 2002, available at www.defenselink.mil/transcripts/transcript.aspx?transcriptid=2610.

3. Transcript of Testimony by Secretary of Defense Donald H. Rumsfeld, House Armed Services Committee, May 07, 2004, available at www.defenselink.mil/speeches/speech.aspx?speechid=117.

4. *Ibid.*

5. Alberto R. Gonzales, "The Rule of Law and the Rules of War," *New York Times*, May 15, 2004.

5. The Center for Constitutional Rights Rebuttal to the Memos and the Torture Program

1. Alberto Gonzales, Memo on "Decision Re Application of the Geneva Convention on Prisoners of War to the Conflict With Al Qaeda and the Taliban," January 25, 2002, available at http://www.slate.com/features/whatistorture/LegalMemos.html (hereafter Memo of January 25th).

2. Art. 60 (5) of the Vienna Convention on the Law of Treaties, 1969, available at http://untreaty.un.org/ilc/texts/instruments/english/conventions/1_1_1969.pdf.

3. 18 USC § 2441 (Supp. III, 1997).

4. John Yoo, Robert J. Delahunty, Memorandum for William J. Haynes II, General Counsel, Department of Defense, Application of Treaties and Laws to al Qaeda and Taliban Detainees, January 9, 2002, at 1;11, available at http://antiwar.com/news/?articleid=2637 (hereafter the Yoo/Delahunty memo).

5. *Ibid.* at 22.

6. *Ibid.*

7. Resolution 1378 of September 14, 2001.

8. Tim Golden, "A Junior Aide Had a Big Role in Terror Policy," *Washington Post,* December 23, 2005, available at www.nytimes.com/2005/12/23/politics/23yoo.html?ex=1292994000&en=a097baececcb7e64&ei=5088&partner=rssnyt&emc=rss.

9. William H. Taft IV, Draft Memorandum to John C. Yoo, January 11, 2002 (copies to Secretary of State and then White House Counsel Gonzales), cover letter at 1, available at www.cartoonbank.com/newyorker/slideshows/01TaftMemo.pdf (hereafter the Taft memo).

10. Art. 60 (5) of the Vienna Convention on the Law of Treaties.

11. Jordan Paust, "Executive Plans and Authorizations to Violate International Law Concerning Treatment and Interrogation of Detainees," *Columbia Journal of Transnational Law* 43, pp. 811–863: ("Although Common Article 3 was developed in 1949 to extend protections to certain persons during an insurgency or armed conflict not of an international character, Common Article 3 now provides a minimum set of customary rights and obligations during any international armed conflict.").

12. "Nazi Conspiracy and Aggression," (Washington, D.C. in United States Government Printing Office, 1946), pp. 528–546.

13. Scott Horton, "A Nuremberg Lesson," *Los Angeles Times*, January 20, 2005.

14. Memorandum of President George W. Bush, February 7, 2002, available at www.washingtonpost.com/wp-srv/nation/documents/020 702bush.pdf.

15. *Ibid.*

16. Memorandum of Jay Bybee and John Yoo, August 1, 2002, (hereafter the torture memo), available at http://news.findlaw.com/up/docs/doj/bybee80102ltr.html.

17. In his sharp questioning of Gonzales during Gonzales's 2005 confirmation hearings as attorney general, Senator Kennedy noted that much of the torture memo's definitions of pain is grounded on "federal statutes that define emergency medical conditions for . . . Medicaid," which "is completely unrelated to the whole questions [of] torture." Alfred W. McCoy, *A Question of Torture: CIA Interrogation, from the Cold War to the War on Terror* (New York: Metropolitan Books, 2006), p. 165.

18. This memo dated December 2004, available at http://fl1.findlaw.com/news.findlaw.com/hdocs/docs/terrorism/dojtorture123004mem .pdf, superseded the torture memo in its entirety. The December 2004 memo critically analyzes the torture memo's statutory interpretation of §§ 2340–40A but does not delve into the torture memo's analysis of the commander-in-chief powers or the necessity/self-defense doctrines. See also Michael C. Dorf, "The Justice Department's Change of Heart Regarding Torture: A Fair-Minded and Praiseworthy Analysis That Could Have Gone Still Further," *FindLaw*, January 5, 2005, available at http://writ.news.findlaw.com/dorf/20050105.html.

19. December 2004 memo at 8, n.17.

20. Torture memo at 22.

21. See www.state.gov/www/global/human_rights/torture_intro.html.

22. United Nations Office of the High Commissioner for Human Rights, "Concluding Observations of the Committee against Torture: Israel." September 5, 1997. Available at www.unhchr.ch/tbs/doc.nsf/0/69b6685c93d9f25180256498005063da?Opendocument.

23. See Geneva Conventions, arts. 3, 5, 27, 31, 32, 33, 147. See also Article 3 of the Inter-American Convention to Prevent and Punish Torture: "The following shall be held guilty of the crime of torture: (a) A public servant or employee who, acting in that capacity, orders, instigates or induces the use of torture, or directly commits it or who, being able to prevent it, fails to do so."

24. Statement of Harold Hongju Koh before the Senate Judiciary Committee regarding the Nomination of the Honorable Alberto R. Gonzales as attorney general of the United States, January 7, 2005, available at www.law.yale.edu/documents/pdf/KohTestimony.pdf.

25. Ibid.

26. *Youngstown Sheet & Tube Co. v. Sawyer, 343 U.S. 579 (1952); United States v. Wappler,* 2 C.M.A. 393 (1953).

27. Available at http://daccessdds.un.org/doc/UNDOC/GEN/G06/432/25/PDF/G0643225.pdf?OpenElement.

28. *United States v. Altstoetter,* Three Trials of War Criminals Before the Nuremberg Military Tribunals Under Control Council Law No. 10 (1951).

29. Telford Taylor, *Final Report to the Secretary of the Army on the Nuernberg* [*sic*] *War Crimes Trials.* (Buffalo, NY: William S. Hein & Co., 1997), p. 172.

30. Ibid.

31. *Prosecutor v. Furundzija,* 38 I.L.M. 317, 367–68 (1999).

32. *Prosecutor v. Krnojelac,* Trial Chamber, March 15, 2002, para. 80.

33. *Tadic* Appeals Judg., July 15, 1999, para. 204 + see 219–220–228.

34. Kai Ambos, *Commentary on the Rome Statute of the International Criminal Court: Observers' Notes, Article by Article,* ed. Otto Triffterer (Baden Baden: Nomos, 1999), p. 480.

35. *Prosecutor v. Blaškić,* Case No. IT-95-14-A. Judgment, 29 July 2004, para. 42.

36. Schlesinger Report, pp. 7–8, 35; See the Fay Report, p. 23 for a list of some of the techniques which required approval, available at http://news.findlaw.com/hdocs/docs/dod/fay82504rpt.pdf; Memorandum from Secretary of Defense Donald Rumsfeld to the Commander of U.S. Southern Command, April 16, 2003.

7. Epilogue: Prosecuting War Crimes

1. Reed Brody and Michael Ratner, eds., *The Pinochet Papers* (Boston: Kluwer Law International, 2000), p. 3.

2. Cf. Richard J. Wilson, "The Spanish Proceedings," in Brody and Ratner, eds., *The Pinochet Papers,* p. 23. Juan Garces's acceptance speech upon receiving the Right Livelihood Award (sometimes called the alternative Nobel Peace Prize) in 1999 can be found at www.tni.org/detail_page.phtml?page=archives_garces_091299.

3. For a careful analysis, see Michael Ratner, "The Lords' Decision in Pinochet III," in Brody and Ratner eds., *The Pinochet Papers,* p. 33.

4. For a book-length discussion of the ripple effect of the Pinochet litigation, see Naomi Roht-Arriaza, *The Pinochet Effect: Transnational Justice in the Age of Human Rights* (Philadelphia: University of Pennsylvania Press, 2005). Cf. also Stacie Jonas, "The Ripple Effect of the Pinochet Case," *American University Washington College of Law Human Rights Brief* 11, no. 3 (Spring 2004), available at www.tni.org/detail_page.phtml?page=archives_jonas_ripple.

5. Besides serious crimes under international law, universal jurisdiction today extends to include crimes such as hijacking and sabotage of aircraft, hostage taking, crimes against internationally protected persons, and apartheid.

6. See Kenneth C. Randall, "Universal Jurisdiction Under International Law," *Texas Law Review*, March 1988, pp. 6–10.

7. Geneva Convention for the Amelioration of the Condition of the Wounded and Sick in Armed Forces in the Field, 75 U.N.T.S. 31, entered into force October 21, 1950, art. 49; Geneva Convention for the Amelioration of the Condition of Wounded, Sick and Shipwrecked Members of Armed Forces at Sea, 75 U.N.T.S. 85, entered into force October 21, 1950, art. 49; Geneva Convention relative to the Treatment of Prisoners of War, 75 U.N.T.S. 135, entered into force October 21, 1950, art. 129; Geneva Convention relative to the Protection of Civilian Persons in Time of War, 75 U.N.T.S. 287, entered into force October 21, 1950, art. 146.

8. For a list of grave breaches see art. 50 GC 1, art. 51 GC 2, art. 130 GC 3, and art. 147 GC 4; available at www.icrc.org/Web/Eng/siteeng0.nsf/html/5ZMGF9 (retrieved September 2007).

9. Convention against Torture and Other Cruel, Inhuman or Degrading Treatment or Punishment, G.A. res. 39/46, [Annex, 39 U.N. GAOR Supp., No. 51, p. 197, U.N. Doc. A/39/51 (1984)], entered into force June 26, 1987, arts. 4–5.

10. International Convention on the Protection of all Persons from Enforced Disappearances, G.A. res. A/RES/61/177, not yet in force, art. 9 (2).

11. Randall, "Universal Jurisdiction," p. 19ff.

12. German Code of Crimes against International Law, § 1, 2002.

13. You can find an English translation of the February 10, 2005, decision at www.brusselstribunal.org/pdf/RumsfeldGermany.pdf.

14. The defendants in the case, U.S. high-ranking officials charged include Former Secretary of Defense Donald Rumsfeld, Former CIA Director George Tenet, Undersecretary of Defense for Intelligence Dr. Stephen Cambone, Lieutenant General Ricardo Sanchez, Major General Geoffrey Miller, Major General Walter Wojdakowski, Colonel Thomas Pappas, Major General Barbara Fast, Colonel Marc Warren, Former Chief White House Counsel Alberto R. Gonzales, General Counsel of the Department of Defense William James Haynes II, Vice President Chief Counsel David S. Addington, Former Deputy Assistant Attorney General John C. Yoo, Former Assistant Attorney General Jay Bybee.